D0651804

HOW
TO BE
EVERYTHING

HOW
TO BE
EVERYTHING

A GUIDE FOR THOSE WHO (STILL)
DON'T KNOW WHAT THEY WANT
TO BE WHEN THEY GROW UP

EMILIE WAPNICK

HarperOne
An Imprint of HarperCollinsPublishers

LIVINGSTON PUBLIC LIBRARY
10 Robert Harp Drive
Livingston, NJ 07039

HOW TO BE EVERYTHING. Copyright © 2017 by Emilie Wapnick. All rights reserved. Printed in the United States of America. No part of this book may be used or reproduced in any manner whatsoever without written permission except in the case of brief quotations embodied in critical articles and reviews. For information, address HarperCollins Publishers, 195 Broadway, New York, NY 10007.

HarperCollins books may be purchased for educational, business, or sales promotional use. For information, please e-mail the Special Markets Department at SPsales@harpercollins.com.

FIRST EDITION

Designed by SBI Book Arts, LLC

Library of Congress Cataloging-in-Publication Data has been applied for.

ISBN 978-0-06-256665-2
ISBN 978-0-06-269797-4 (international)

17 18 19 20 21   LSC   10 9 8 7 6 5 4 3 2 1

FOR VALERIE

Artistry trumps mastery.

—MAGGIE NELSON

CONTENTS

Part III

COMMON MULTIPOTENTIALITE STUMBLING BLOCKS

SLAYING YOUR DRAGONS

PREFACE

A LETTER TO THE READER

If you picked up this book, it's probably because you've had trouble narrowing down "what you want to be" to one thing. I'm not going to show you how to do that.

This book is for the people who don't want to pick a single focus and abandon all their other interests. It's for the curious, for those who find delight in learning new things, creating and morphing between identities.

You don't have to choose one thing. That's the big secret no one tells you. This book will show you how to build a sustainable and fruitful career that will allow you to explore to your heart's content—to BE EVERYTHING.

Be warned, however. This is no ordinary book. And it's no ordinary reading experience. Building a multifaceted life takes introspection and experimentation. I'll be here to guide you, but I'm going to ask you to do some things along the way. They may or may not include the following: making a lot of lists, throwing tantrums, researching strange combinations of words. . . . So grab a pen, some paper, and perhaps a snazzy highlighter to mark the sentences you want to remember. This is the start of something big. And really fun.

PART I

EVERYTHING?

WELCOME TO THE TRIBE

THERE IS NOTHING WRONG WITH YOU

"Emilie?"

I lifted my eyes from the menu at the deli. Standing before me was the acting teacher I'd studied with as a teenager. It had been years since I'd last seen her. We hugged and caught up a little, and she told me about how her theater school was going.

"And what are you up to these days?" she asked.

"I'm about to start law school in the fall," I replied enthusiastically. (Since taking an introductory law class the year before, I'd developed a nerdy fascination with things like contracts and property law. These systems felt like an entirely new way of looking at the world.)

Her reaction was not what I expected. A funny expression materialized on her face, as she cocked her head to one side.

"Hm. I thought you were going to be a filmmaker."

My heart sunk. There it was: my problem, verbalized in a single sentence.

I thought you were going to be a filmmaker.

This happened nearly a decade ago. I was twenty-three, and I was slowly beginning to observe a pattern in myself. I noticed my tendency to dive into a new field, become completely engrossed, voraciously devour every bit of related information I could get my hands on, and complete a few projects I was very passionate about. After a number of months (or years), my interest would miraculously begin to wane and I would shift toward a new and exciting field, at which point the pattern would repeat. Boredom always set in once I reached a fairly high level of proficiency. Of course, this was also the point at which people would look at me and say: "Wow, Emilie, you're good at this! You've really found your thing, haven't you?" Ugh. Cue the guilt. Cue the shame.

This way of being in the world—becoming fascinated by something, diving in, gaining skills, and losing interest—caused me a lot of anxiety. Assuming that the tendency to pivot between disciplines was unique to me, I felt totally alone. My peers certainly didn't have everything figured out, but they all seemed to be on a linear trajectory toward something. My path, on the other hand, was just a mess of zigzags: music, art, web design, filmmaking, law . . .

When my former acting teacher told me, with apparent confusion and disappointment, that she THOUGHT I WAS GOING TO BE A FILMMAKER, it was like I crashed face-first into a Truth about myself that I'd been hiding from: I was incapable of sticking with anything. That moment felt like a moment of clarity, and it did not feel good. A million questions spun in my head: *Will I ever find my Thing? Do I even have a Thing? If my calling isn't any of the Things I've tried before, will it be the next one? Will I ever be content in one job for more than a few years, or will each profession eventually lose its luster?* And the most cutting question of all: *If I must flit between fields in order to stay happy, will I ever amount to anything?* I worried that I was, at my core, someone who couldn't commit or follow through. I was certain that there was something wrong with me.

Someone might label these thoughts frivolous, privileged, or a product of my age or (lack of) maturity at the time, but "Why am I here?" is a question that humans of all ages grapple with. The experience of this kind of confusion—confusion around not just career, but *identity* itself—feels anything but frivolous. It is paralyzing.

WHAT DO YOU WANT TO BE WHEN YOU GROW UP?

Do you remember being asked, as a little kid, what you wanted to be when you grew up? How did you feel? When I think back to when I was five or six, I don't remember my specific answer. But I do remember what happened after I answered: the face of the adult who had asked took on a look of approval and pride. It felt good to declare an identity. The world (well, my little world, at least) approved.

Something happens to many of us as we get older: "What do you want to be when you grow up?" goes from being a fun exercise in daydreams to a more serious, more anxiety-inducing question. We begin to feel the pressure to respond with a practical answer: one with weight and consequences, to which we will be held. We sense the people around us trying to pinpoint the type of person we are becoming, and we want the same kind of approval we were granted as little kids when we declared our desire to become circus clowns or dinosaurs.

We want all of this, but we don't want to be boxed in or to make the wrong choice. While outside forces prod us to "declare a major," "home in on our strengths," and "find a niche," we mortals are struggling to understand who we are and what kind of significance our life will have. It's a mess of external and internal pressures, intertwined with existential and identity confusion. This mess isn't relegated to adolescence, either. For many of us, it continues throughout our lives.

THE MYTH OF THE ONE TRUE CALLING

One reason that "What do you want to be . . ." has the ability to wreak havoc in our hearts and psyches is that it implies the need to be *one thing*. There's a good chance that if your five-year-old self rattled off a list of ten different future selves, the adult posing the question would say something like, "Well, which is it? You can't be all of those!" Certainly, once we reach adolescence, there's far less tolerance for answers like, "I'm going to be a marine biologist, textile artist, and journalist!" It's subtle, but we can translate *What do you want to be when you grow up?* to *You are allowed one identity in this life, so which is it?* How terrifying is that? When phrased that way, it's no wonder the question stresses us out.

The message that we must decide on a single identity is reinforced in many contexts. Mainstream career books and guidance counselors give us tests to help us whittle down our career options to the perfect fit. Colleges and universities ask us to declare a major. Employers sometimes ask applicants to explain ourselves when we possess skills in outside fields, implying we lack focus or ability. We receive ominous warnings from the people in our lives and the media about the dangers of being a quitter, a flake, or a jack-of-all-trades, master of none. A specialized life is portrayed as the only path to success, and it's highly romanticized in our culture. We've all heard of the doctor who always knew she wanted to be a doctor, or the writer who wrote his first novel at the age of ten. These people are held up as shining examples for the rest of us, and—while people like this certainly exist (no hate intended to the focused few!)—many of us simply don't fit into their model. Through social cues and conditioning, we learn to believe in the romantic notion of the One True Calling: the idea that we each have one great thing we are meant to do with our life—OUR DESTINY!

What happens if you don't fit into this framework? Let's say you're curious about several subjects, and there are many things you'd like to do with your life. If you're unable or unwilling to settle on a single career path, you might worry that you don't have One True Calling like everybody else, and that, therefore, your life lacks purpose.

It doesn't. In fact, there is a very good reason for your tendency to shift between things, to devour new knowledge and experiences, and to try on new identities.

YOU ARE A MULTIPOTENTIALITE

Have you been nodding your head along as you read? Good news! You are probably a multipotentialite: someone with many interests and creative pursuits.[1] If this is the first time you've encountered the word, it might seem like a mouthful. Try breaking *multipotentialite* up into three parts, and saying it aloud slowly: *multi—potential—ite*. And, again: *multi—potential—ite*. Not so bad, right? Well, in any case, if you have a hard time with *multipotentialite* or it doesn't feel like a good fit for you, there are other options. Here are the most common terms for the kind of person we're talking about:

- Multipotentialite: someone with many interests and creative pursuits

- Polymath: someone who knows a lot about many different things or a person of encyclopedic learning

- Renaissance Person: a person who is interested in and knows a lot about many things

- Jack-of-All-Trades: a person who can do passable work at various tasks; a handy, versatile person

- Generalist: one whose skills, interests, or habits are varied or unspecialized

- Scanner: someone with intense curiosity about numerous unrelated subjects (coined by Barbara Sher in her great book *Refuse to Choose!*)

1. In other words, multiple potentials.

- Puttylike (adj.): able to embody different identities and perform a variety of tasks gracefully

These synonyms have slight differences in meaning. *Multipotentialite* and *Scanner* emphasize drive and curiosity, while *Polymath* and *Renaissance Person* emphasize accumulated knowledge (and have historical connotations as well—they may evoke names such as Leonardo da Vinci and Benjamin Franklin). *Jack-of-All-Trades* tends to refer to someone's skills rather than their knowledge, and *Generalist* implies someone with broad but shallow knowledge. The differences are subtle. Ultimately, what matters is that whatever word you adopt for yourself feels right. Use the term(s) that resonate most, use no term at all, or invent your own.[2]

WHAT KIND OF MULTIPOTENTIALITE ARE YOU?

There is no single way to be a multipotentialite. Some of us have a dozen projects on the go at once, others prefer to dive into a single subject for months or years, making it our sole focus until we switch to a new area entirely. A multipotentialite's interests can occur simultaneously (several interests at one time), sequentially (one interest at a time), or anywhere in between.

SIMULTANEOUS ←————————————————→ SEQUENTIAL
(Many projects at a time)   (One project at a time)

---

2. It is somewhat appropriate that, as a community, we are unable to agree on a single label.

To figure out your own place on this spectrum, think about your past interests, projects, and jobs. Notice any patterns? Do you tend to be interested in many different topics at once, or do you prefer to focus intently on one thing at a time before moving on to the next one (and then the next)? How many projects do you like to have on your plate at once, and how many is too many? Perhaps your capacity for taking on projects is like a stove: you have four pots on four burners; some are boiling on high while others simmer in the back. Maybe your metaphorical stove is more like the industrial range in a restaurant, with a griddle and an infinite number of projects sizzling away. Alternatively, maybe you have a campfire that produces one glorious blaze at a time.

Most of us actually fall somewhere in the middle of the simultaneous–sequential spectrum, and we often move along it at different points in our life. If you have no idea where you fall, don't freak out! We'll figure it out together. Our interests are sometimes fleeting, and they sometimes never leave us. They can also fade, only to reemerge years later. It doesn't matter how you move through your various interests and passions; all methods of being a multipotentialite are equally valid.

A MULTIPOTENTIALITE'S ROAD MAP (HINT: IT'S NOT A STRAIGHT LINE)

We are taught that each field of interest points in one direction, leading to an associated career. Let's say that you're a scientifically inclined high school student. You might go on to study biology in college, pursue a premed track, go to medical school, complete your residency, and then become a doctor. Sure, there are different types of doctors. You might eventually practice, teach, or do research, but it's generally assumed that a med student will use the skills acquired in their studies in service of the associated career: doctor. The same is true of other fields. Surely, an architecture student will become an architect, and a music major will become a musician (or maybe a music teacher). An engineering student is expected to become an engineer. Each of these fields has an associated career at the end of a vertical trajectory.[3] A specialist might go straight down any one of these trajectories to the associated career, but multipotentialites are different. We move both vertically *and* laterally. We apply skills beyond service of their associated career, to other disciplines, and in unusual ways.

Let's use my own path for example. Music, art, film, and law are four fields that I pursued, either professionally or academically. Consider the vertical trajectory of each field (see example on page 12).

Theoretically, I could have gone straight down any of these trajectories. I promise that I tried, but I just couldn't do it! My path looked more like the example on page 13.

It's a bit of a mess, isn't it? I don't regret pursuing any of these fields, although I never became a full-time musician, web designer, filmmaker, or lawyer. Learning about interesting stuff is inherently joyful and I've found that many skills gained in these pursuits have helped me across different contexts. My legal education made me a more persuasive writer, a skill I use

3. When people refer to so-called useless majors, they are often talking about fields like English or philosophy, which have fewer careers vertically associated with them. I don't believe in useless majors. The skills acquired in programs like these often end up being applied in different fields altogether.

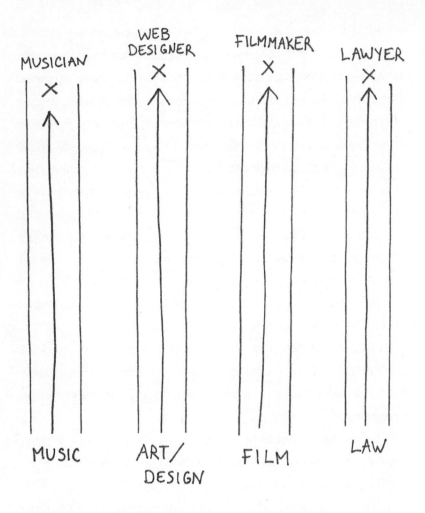

every time I write a blog post, fill out an application, or draft a proposal of any kind. The years I spent immersed in the music scene and playing in a band taught me how to work well on teams, which I use every day in my business. Playing in a band also gave me valuable performance experience, which helped with public speaking years later. My background in web design allows me to build websites for any of my projects or to communicate effectively with a designer, if I choose to hire one. And there's nothing quite like producing short films to teach you

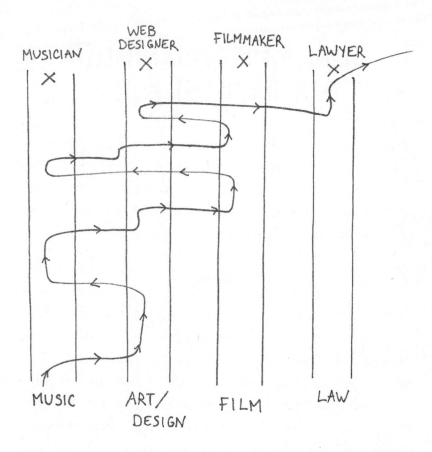

about the complexities of event planning and the dynamics of working with different (and difficult) personalities. Most of my "past lives" have been useful in real and practical ways. I do occasionally use my skills as expected, like building a website for a client or getting paid to play music, but I more frequently apply them laterally, in contexts where they can build on one another. Can you think of times when you applied your skills in surprising ways? For example, maybe playing the piano made you a faster typist. Or maybe working with animals taught you to be a more empathetic teacher. Is this starting to make a whole lot of sense? Our paths may look random or chaotic on paper, but they are often more practical than we think.

BEING A MULTIPOTENTIALITE IN A SPECIALIST WORLD

Being a multipotentialite is wonderful, and embracing your many passions rocks! However, being blessed with this particular psychological makeup also presents certain challenges. Multipotentialites tend to struggle with three main areas: work, productivity, and self-esteem.

Work

Finding meaningful and sustainable work can be one of our greatest challenges. Upon discovering our multipotentiality, many of us find that years of worry and confusion instantly fall away. However, a big, ominous question tends to follow the realization. *Phew, I'm a multipotentialite, great! But, now, how the heck will I make a living?* The idea of doing one thing forever can sound like a nightmare to us, but financial instability due to regularly jumping ship can sound just as terrifying. Is there an alternative to these two approaches? Is there a way to make "the multipotentialite thing" work? That is the central question of this book. In the chapters to come, we'll meet multipotentialites who are both happy and financially comfortable. We'll learn about how they structure their careers to support their multipotentiality, and how you can do the same.

Productivity

While productivity is a challenge for most people, it is essential that those of us pursuing multiple projects figure out our own personal productivity system. How do you focus on several projects at once and make progress on all of them? How do you deal with the internal muck (procrastination, self-doubt, overwhelm, and chronic e-mail checking) that can prevent you from moving forward with your goals? In Chapter 8, we'll take a look at some tools that will help you choose what to focus on, decide how to structure your time, and know when to change directions. We'll also discuss techniques for overcoming procrastination and getting into the flow.

Self-Esteem

The modern world isn't always friendly to multipotentialites. As a result, many of us grow up with feelings of self-doubt, low self-esteem, and other mental health issues. Multipotentiality in teens is associated with depression, anxiety, overwhelm, existential dilemmas, and guilt about the inability to choose or about changing directions.[4] These feelings can persist into adulthood, causing a lot of pain, and holding us back from stepping into our potentials. In Chapter 9, we'll address these issues by considering our most common insecurities:

- Guilt and shame (when moving from an area to the next)

- The discomfort of being a beginner again and again

- The fear of not being the best

- Imposter syndrome

- External critics

- The dreaded *So, what do you do?*

4. Check out the Notes and Selected Further Reading section on page 215 for a little slice of the current research.

We will discuss each of these challenges—work, productivity, and self-esteem—in depth. As we do, you'll begin putting together your own personalized plan of action. Armed with the information in this book, my hope is that you will begin to design a life that allows you to be the biggest, best multipotentialite you can be—to be fully you, and to have a career and life that is aligned with how you are wired. I hope this not only for the sake of your happiness, but so that the rest of us might benefit from the amazing work you will do over the course of your life.

The truth is that you aren't lacking a destiny or purpose. There is a very good reason for your insatiable curiosity: you're someone who's going to shake things up, create something novel, solve complex, multidimensional problems, make people's lives better in your own unique way. Whatever your destinies are, you can't step into them while stifling your multipotentiality. You must embrace it and use it.

2

MULTIPOTENTIALITES: SLACKERS OR INNOVATORS?

You're probably familiar with the common perception of those who do many things: that we are slackers whose inability to commit to one thing is our fatal flaw. Almost every language, from Arabic to Korean, has a version of the expression "jack-of-all-trades, master of none." The Spanish phrase *Quien mucho abarca poco aprieta* means "He who embraces too much has a weak grasp." In Lithuanian, the sentence *Devyni amatai, dešimtas badas* means something like "When you have nine trades, then your tenth one is starvation." The Vietnamese saying *Một nghề cho chín, còn hơn chín nghề* gets right to the heart of the judgments against us: "Being a master in one job is better than being average in nine jobs." But are multipotentialites really *average* at our jobs? Are we actually unknowledgeable, and suffering financially because of it? Let's dive into the jack-of-all-trades, master-of-none argument, and see how it holds up in practice.

"DOING MANY THINGS MEANS BEING MEDIOCRE AT ALL OF THEM"

This argument seems to make sense from a mathematical perspective: If person A puts ten thousand hours[1] into learning a single trade, and person B spends twenty-five hundred hours learning four different trades, then person B is bound to be less "skilled" (i.e., more mediocre) in any given field, right? This argument is based on the idea that *skill* is the only quality that matters. I want to make the argument that creativity, ingenuity, and passion are equally important. Does someone with decades of musical training necessarily write more beautiful (or even more profitable) songs than a musician who has been playing for just a few years? Is a seasoned high school teacher more effective than a teacher who is just a few years

1. Malcolm Gladwell popularized the "ten-thousand-hour rule" in his book *Outliers*. The rule is that it takes ten thousand hours of practice to become a world-class performer. This theory was based on research by psychologist Anders Ericsson, which looked at the practice habits of world-class athletes and musical virtuosos. Since the release of *Outliers* the ten-thousand-hour rule has been expanded from its original meaning, applied to contexts where it was never meant to be applied, and interpreted in ways that go beyond the scope of the original research. It is now commonly used to suggest that individuals shouldn't pursue something unless they are willing to invest ten thousand hours. In my opinion, this interpretation devalues anything other than technical ability and discourages learning and exploration. For a powerful response to the ten-thousand-hour rule, check out Josh Kaufman's book *The First 20 Hours*.

into their career but is brimming with enthusiasm and passion for their work? The answer in both of these cases is no—or rather, *not necessarily*. Expertise matters, but it isn't the sole factor in gauging our future success, career happiness, or social contributions.

Specialists and Generalists Are Both Needed, but Often in Different Contexts

A high level of technical skill matters more in certain fields and positions than it does in others. Heart surgeons are highly specialized for good reason. I don't know about you, but I would certainly prefer to have a specialist operating on my heart! When it comes to the treatment of chronic health issues, on the other hand, I am more interested in working with a practitioner who is less specialized and has a real grasp of how the different systems of the body work together. It took me a while to find my current doctor. He's a board-certified naturopath, as well as a licensed acupuncturist and functional medicine practitioner. This means that he has a number of different tools at his disposal. When dealing with a health issue, he always suggests the treatment that "works and causes the least amount of harm." In some cases this involves the use of prescription drugs, but in many others, it's an herbal protocol or dietary change that best fits these criteria. This approach isn't for everyone, but it works for me. However, like I said, if I ever need heart surgery, you can bet I'll be asking my doc for a referral (and I'm quite sure he'll be happy to give me one)! Specialists and generalists are both valuable and necessary; it just depends on the context.

Not Being "The Best"
Isn't the Same as Being Mediocre

There is a middle ground between being world class and utterly mediocre. Although some of our interests are short-lived, multipotentialites are often highly skilled in a few areas. We may even be experts! A more accurate, albeit less pithy, expression to describe a multipotentialite might be: "jack-of-many-trades, master of some." That said, it's possible to make and do outstanding work by being proficient *enough* in a given area and combining that skill with creativity and passion.

Multipotentialites Define
Our Own Categories

Take a look at your book collection or library checkout history. There's a good chance that you don't just read books about single topics (math, music, politics, philosophy). You probably also love titles that are amalgamations of multiple topics. Scanning my bookshelf right now, I see books that are about the relationships between disciplines: architecture and psychology, math and color, the philosophy of walking. I also see genre-bending books such as poetry-memoirs and a comedic book about anxiety. These books have to have been written by multipotentialites. While specialists excel in a single domain, multipotentialites blend domains together and work in the intersections. This allows us to achieve a deep level of knowledge on *the relationship between domains*—our own form of expertise.

MULTIPOTENTIALITE SUPERPOWERS

Okay, I'm done defending us against accusations of mediocrity. Here is the interesting question: How can multipotentialites lead with our strengths? If you're anything like the multipotentialites I know, you've spent far too long worrying about whether you are doomed. It's time to put that disempowering rhetoric aside and consider an alternative: maybe multipotentialites are just misunderstood movers and shakers. And maybe we have our own set of strengths: our superpowers! Let's take a look at five things that multipotentialites do extremely well and let's meet some people who are putting their superpowers to good use.

Multipotentialite Superpower #1: Idea Synthesis

We are excellent synthesizers. Combining two or more concepts and creating something new at the intersection is totally our jam. Twig Terrariums is a florist's shop in Brooklyn that specializes in living sculptures. Imagine a glass jar, vase, orb, or beaker that houses moss, succulents, flowers, and . . . tiny, hand-painted figurines. Each creation tells a different story: an elderly couple sitting on a bench, a cowboy herding cattle, a zombie apocalypse, a punk rocker raising a bottle of booze and giving the world the finger. Twig was founded by friends Michelle Inciarrano and Katy Maslow, who combined their interests in science, botany, storytelling, art, and design to create something unique. With the help of Michelle's chemistry professor (Michelle was a science student at the time—talk about lateral skill application!), the pair engineered a successful ecosystem in a cruet jar from Michelle's kitchen cabinet. From there, they began experimenting with different types of terrariums, and eventually Twig Terrariums was born.

Idea synthesis can result in something totally original. By extension, it can be used to address pressing social problems with totally original solutions. Between 2004 and 2013, according to State of Utah reports, chronic homelessness dropped in the state by 91 percent. This remarkable decline is attributed to a model called Housing First, which was developed by clinical psychologist Sam Tsemberis through his Pathways to Housing program. Under the Housing First approach, chronically homeless people are provided with homes without meeting any preconditions. Giving homes to the homeless might not sound revolutionary, but it (weirdly) defies conventional wisdom in the field. Under the previous antihomelessness model in Utah, chronically homeless people were required to be sober and drug-free before qualifying for housing. Tsemberis's model provides people with roofs over their heads first and social services second. The Housing First approach has been tested in rural and urban settings across America with similarly impressive results.

One of the most interesting aspects of this story is that Tsemberis did not have training in homeless services; he was a psychologist. In the early 1990s, Tsemberis worked at an organization that did outreach for mentally ill people. He ended up working closely with homeless people and learning about the incredible challenges of living on the street. He found himself treating the same people again and again, and it became obvious to him that the current model wasn't working. Tsemberis developed the Housing First model by drawing from his training and experience as a psychologist. He started from the premise that it is difficult to address addiction and mental illness without first reducing the extreme stress and instability that come with living on the street.

It is often outsiders, rather than seasoned experts, who come up with solutions to long-standing problems. As Dr. Karim Lakhani and Dr. Lars Bo Jeppesen explain in the *Harvard Business Review,* "The more diverse the problem-solving population, the more likely a problem is to be solved. People tend to link problems that are distant from their fields with solutions they've encountered in their own work." Multipotentialites are in a great position to come up with creative solutions because we have so many perspectives to draw from. We're a "diverse problem-solving population" all in one!

Multipotentialite Superpower #2: Rapid Learning

Multipotentialites grasp concepts and pick up skills quickly for three main reasons:

1. We understand how it feels to be a beginner (i.e., to fumble around in the dark). Knowing that we've overcome the awkward beginner stage before means we're less discouraged when we encounter it again. With each area that we master, we gain confidence in our ability to absorb and understand new things. This confidence, in turn, accelerates learning by making us more likely to take creative risks and step out of our comfort zones.

2. We are passionate (almost obsessional at times) about the things that fascinate us. Our passion drives us to absorb as much as we can in a short period of time. We've been known to lose hours to research, speed-read books, and deeply immerse ourselves in new activities.[2]

3. We rarely start from scratch when pursuing a new interest, since many skills are transferable across disciplines. Your knowledge of math, for example, might help you grasp music theory more quickly. And years of writing poetry, engrossing yourself in the problem of how words work in relationship to each other, might make it easier to learn how to code.

Rapid learning is awesome, especially in the workplace. Television advertising producer Tom Vaughan-Mountford was able to teach himself WordPress and Google AdWords in order to build a new corporate website for the company he works for. His ability to acquire skills quickly meant that his company didn't have to hire an outside developer, which would have cost them thousands of dollars. Beyond the skills themselves, the simple willingness to try new things can also make multipotentialites very popular at work. Consultant JB Fournier found this to be true at his last job:

> I was hired by a large consulting firm. As time went by, I slowly became the go-to person for stuff nobody quite knew how to do. I was known for "giving it a shot,"

2. Sound familiar?

whatever "it" may have been. My talent was to disregard the hesitation that my highly specialized colleagues felt towards the unknown, namely the sentiment: if you've never done something, then you probably should not attempt it.

Intellectual curiosity is a staple of multipotentiality, so it's rare to find a multipotentialite who isn't interested in learning.[3] Many people assume that we stop learning once we reach a certain age or leave school, but research has shown that it's possible to learn at any age. Yet, when discussing cognitive performance, neuroscientists have coined something called the "use it or lose it" principle: if you don't use a particular skill (or part of the brain) on a regular basis, you will have a harder time tapping into it in the future. If you aren't used to learning new things regularly through self-study or formal education, you might be a little rusty at it. But with time and practice you can develop your ability to learn, and learn quickly.

Multipotentialite Superpower #3: Adaptability

Multipotentialites can make ourselves at home in many settings and roles. We can draw from our vast and varied skill sets, depending on the needs of our employers, clients, or customers.

3. There are a few exceptions to this. A multipotentialite who is suffering from depression might not feel interested in learning, since depression can hinder one's motivation. And for someone whose economic situation or responsibilities make it difficult to prioritize learning over getting food on the table, it might be far from the front of their mind.

As the programs coordinator at a school, Carli F. finds that she morphs between the roles of adviser, mentor, liaison, teacher, facilitator, writer, logistics director, marketer, and technology assistant, sometimes all in the same day. The ability to do many things and switch dexterously between activities can make us both indispensable and difficult to replace.

Adaptability is an asset to multipotentialites who are free-lancers and business owners. Abe Cajudo is a web designer, video director, and creative consultant. He works with small businesses, artists, and educational organizations on a range of tasks, including design work, crowd-funding campaigns, and online course creation. Abe has clients who know him strictly as a web designer and others who know him as a video producer. It isn't uncommon for past clients to learn about the range of his abilities and to hire him in an additional capacity. Many of his past clients are surprised and delighted to find out that he can help them with another part of their project.

Being adaptable makes us more resilient in an unstable and quickly evolving economy. By having multiple revenue streams, we can avoid putting all our eggs in one basket. If the demand for our landscaping services wanes, we can take on more pro-gramming work. If we get laid off from our job as a tour guide, we can look for work in the tourism industry or apply for jobs in all the other fields in which we have interest or experience. Robert Safian, the editor and managing director for *Fast Com-pany,* explains that the key to thriving in an uncertain economy is having "a mind-set that embraces instability, that tolerates—and even enjoys—recalibrating careers, business models and assumptions." In the postrecession era, adaptability is not merely an asset; it's a necessity.

Multipotentialite Superpower #4: Big-Picture Thinking

Multipotentialites are able to see how individual ideas connect to the wider world. We are big-picture thinkers who enjoy brainstorming, conceiving of lofty projects, and thinking up ways in which we can make things better. Douglas Tsoi saw a need for more affordable and accessible education in his home of Portland, Oregon. The demand he observed for low-cost education, along with his own love of learning, prompted Douglas to found Portland Underground Grad School, which provides graduate-level education at affordable prices. The course offerings are varied, with titles like: Gender and Digital Identity; Genetics, Genomics, and Genethics; and From the Political Marionette to Jim Henson: The Importance of Puppets. They offer scholarships to people who need them and ask students who can afford it to make a voluntary contribution to the scholarship fund.

As multipotentialites learn about different facets of the world, we begin to see how subjects relate to and interact with one another. Our broad perspective allows us to spot systemic problems that specialists, with their deep understanding of a single area, might miss. And our understanding of how choices impact other sectors allows us to come up with more compassionate and better-informed solutions. Douglas recognized that the price of postsecondary education in the United States is a barrier for many people who wish to learn. But instead of just accepting this as *the way things are,* he used his creativity and connections to mobilize a different kind of educational system—one that is open, accessible, and community-based.

The ability to zoom out and consider problems holistically is an asset in the workplace. It allows us to anticipate both opportunities and potential problems, analyze information, and stay ahead of the curve.

If you want to flex your Big Idea muscles at work, work for a company that is interested in the ideas and opinions of its employees. We'll be talking about the sorts of organizations and positions that are well suited to multipotentialites in the upcoming chapters, but in the meantime, remember that receptivity to new ideas and to employee input is something to look for when considering prospective employers.

Multipotentialite Superpower #5: Relating and Translating

Multipotentialites are natural connectors, both in the sense that we love connecting with people on an emotional level, and in that we love helping people understand and connect with one another. (We also love connecting ideas, as we previously discussed.) Our varied experiences give us the ability to relate to people from different walks of life, and our intense curiosity makes us good listeners. To a multipotentialite, there's nothing quite like nerding out about our latest obsession with someone who shares it, especially if that person happens to be an expert and can help us deepen our knowledge.

Taken a step further, the ability to relate to different types of people means that we can help people relate to one another by translating between them. Multipotentialites often find ourselves interacting with specialists at work, and our ability to converse in each of their "languages" is an incredible asset. As a theater technician, Julia Junghans often finds herself acting as a liaison between different types of specialists:

> My many interests and experiences help me initiate healthy dialogue between two parties that may have trouble communicating because of their different realms of expertise. For instance, designers and technicians have quite a different language they use when talking about producing a theater work. I have been on both sides, and I have worked outside the theater industry so I am a good "translator."

In her book *Refuse to Choose!,* author Barbara Sher likens the Scanner (or multipotentialite) to an orchestra conductor. The example works both literally and metaphorically. A conductor has (at minimum) basic training in several instruments, so she knows how to communicate with each section to help them understand the tonal and rhythmic qualities she is seeking. She can ask the violinists to play on a certain part of the bow to get the right sound for a passage, or help the percussionists with a particularly tricky entrance. And, when the orchestra begins to play, the conductor facilitates the way the different sections of the orchestra blend together and "speak" to one another, bringing a bigger vision to light. Multipotentialites are often described as "bridge builders" or "hubs of the wheel," because of how easily we communicate with and lead multidisciplinary teams.

TAPPING INTO YOUR SUPERPOWERS

Although many multipotentialites are adept at these five superpowers, some of us are more practiced than others and have an easier time applying them. I occasionally receive an e-mail from someone who spent most of their life trying (miserably) to specialize—not because they had genuine interest in a single area, but because that was what they thought they *should* be doing. These e-mails are usually doused in regret and frustration, but they generally contain a kernel of hope for what might be if they begin to embrace, rather than fight, their plurality. I've received e-mails like this from people of all ages: from twenty-somethings to people in their seventies. It's never too late to get started. The more you allow yourself to explore, draw connections between different ideas, dream up big projects, and collaborate with others, the stronger your superpowers will become. You might even discover that you have a few more!

THE RELATIONSHIP BETWEEN MULTIPOTENTIALITY AND INNOVATION

Multipotentialites have always been innovators, and innovators have often been multipotentialites.[4] Aristotle was trained as a physician before becoming a philosopher. Benjamin Franklin invented the lightning rod and bifocals in addition to being a politician (among other things). Leonardo da Vinci, the best-known polymath of all time, was an accomplished artist, inventor, and mathematician (again, among other things). Is there

---

4. Check out Appendix A to learn about more famous multipotentialites.

something about being interested in many things that makes us predisposed to innovation?

Although mainstream culture tries to paint us as dilettantes, the reality is that when we make use of our strengths, multipotentialites can thrive professionally and contribute to the world in refreshingly original ways. As Adam Grant, author of *Originals: How Non-Conformists Move the World,* explained in a piece in the *New York Times,* there's a strong correlation between having many interests and producing innovative work:

> Evidence shows that creative contributions depend on the breadth, not just depth, of our knowledge and experience. In fashion, the most original collections come from directors who spend the most time working abroad. In science, winning a Nobel Prize is less about being a single-minded genius and more about being interested in many things. Relative to typical scientists, Nobel Prize winners are 22 times more likely to perform as actors, dancers or magicians; 12 times more likely to write poetry, plays or novels; seven times more likely to dabble in arts and crafts; and twice as likely to play an instrument or compose music.

As we've seen, multipotentialites are creative, out-of-the-box thinkers, who can learn quickly and adapt to fluctuating times and circumstances. We're passionate, we love tackling problems and connecting with our fellow humans, and we're good at leading interdisciplinary teams. This isn't to say that we don't face challenges or have weaknesses, but given our natural inclinations, it's not surprising that multipotentialites tend to be the ones shaking things up.

THE REAL PROBLEM

When it comes to professional success, the biggest thing that gets in our way isn't flakiness; it's a lack of resources. Specialists are equipped with innumerable career books, counselors who understand them, and a linear educational system that was built just for them. Of course, professional happiness doesn't always come easily to specialists, either. It can take them time to figure out in which industry they'd like to build a career. Nevertheless, specialist structures and values are widely understood and respected. Nobody hurls accusations of "one trick pony-ism" at specialists and suggests that they kindly add another major to their degree. Where are the resources for those of us who are wired a little differently and don't want to be *just* one thing?

My hope is that you're holding one in your hand. I put this book together so that people like us would have somewhere to turn when designing their careers and their lives. Throughout the next few chapters, we'll be getting into the nitty-gritty, practical stuff. How exactly do we design careers that allow us to tap into our multipotentialite superpowers? How do we make sense of and balance the many things we want to do? If multipotentialites don't have clear, predefined career paths, the way many specialists do, then where do we even start? Get ready; it's time to get to work.

THE COMPONENTS OF A HAPPY MULTIPOTENTIALITE LIFE

What is the ideal career for a multipotentialite? Should we become architects, since architecture will allow us to use both sides of our brains and blend together the arts and sciences? Is project management the way to go, since it will let us focus on many things at once? Should we just reject traditional employment altogether and be our own bosses for maximum freedom and flexibility? Unfortunately, there isn't a single career path that is perfect for all multipotentialites.[1] There are plenty of

1. Duh.

multipotentialites who have fulfilling professional lives as architects, project managers, and entrepreneurs, but many others for whom these careers would be a terrible fit. Although we may share an intense curiosity about numerous topics, multipotentialites are all different, and we each have our own interests, values, and priorities.

The truth, which I begrudgingly discovered while interviewing people for this book, is that happy multipotentialites can be found in any role and every industry, including some seemingly specialist ones. A pilot, for instance, might appear to be a specialist, but if you zoom out you'll see that she is also a filmmaker and activist. Consider the architectural drafter with a previous career in education, who will go on to open a restaurant. If this person were to be asked the question "So, what do you do?" at a party, they might answer, "I'm an architectural drafter." Right then, you might consider them to be fairly narrowly focused, but with all the facts it's clear that they are, in fact, a multipotentialite who moves through their interests sequentially.

Here's the problem: if multipotentialites are able to thrive in an infinite number of professions, and what works for one person doesn't necessarily work for the next, then where should we begin when designing our careers? To answer this question, I surveyed and interviewed hundreds of multipotentialites who self-describe as being both happy and financially comfortable. I wanted to know how they do it. Although the interviewees and survey participants had radically different careers, they shared a few important similarities. They had all designed lives that provided them with three common elements: *money, meaning,* and *variety*—in the amounts that were right for them.

THIS IS ABOUT LIFE DESIGN, NOT CAREER PLANNING

As I learned more about the participants' stories, I realized that their sense of fulfillment doesn't stem solely from their careers. What they do to make money is just one piece of the equation—a piece that fits into a broader life they have intentionally created. In other words, this book is not about career planning. It's about life design. That's why it's titled *How to Be Everything,* and not *How to Make a Living Doing Everything*.

We will meet people in the upcoming chapters who have found money, meaning, and variety in a single job. We will also meet people who are just as satisfied getting some of these elements through their career and some through a colorful array of hobbies and personal projects. Individual preference and the nature of our interests play a big part in how we choose to structure our lives and our careers. Ultimately, the important thing is that money, meaning, and variety are present in your life as a whole. Your career should be aligned with your overall goals. Your work should feel like an integrated and supportive force in your life, not the kind-of-awful-thing-you-have-to-do-to-pay-the-bills. With that said, let's dive into each element to learn more.

1. MONEY

Hello, emotional baggage! This is a tough topic. Many of us hold beliefs about money that we picked up from our parents and/or society. We may have internalized the idea that there is never enough of it, that money equals happiness, or that our paycheck is representative of our value in the world. Capitalist culture can encourage an unhealthy attitude around money. The idea of the "hustle" is romanticized, which can make us feel like we need to work all the time in order to succeed. There is a considerable body of evidence that overwork is detrimental to our health. Long working hours are associated with stress, anxiety disorders, depression, insomnia, type 2 diabetes, and cardiovascular disease. However, while overwork is a serious problem, the need for money taps into our very survival instincts. It's real. We need money for food and shelter, so a perceived lack of it can trigger biological responses like "fight or flight," whether or not we're truly at imminent risk.

The Ingredient Approach to Money

Whatever your beliefs or issues around money—however essential or superfluous you consider it to be—most of us can agree that some amount of money is necessary. A helpful way to look at the need for money is what author John Armstrong calls the "ingredient approach." Money can be seen as *but one* ingredient in a happy life. On its own, money isn't enough. But when money is combined with other virtues (defined as "good abilities of mind and character"), it can empower us to meet our goals. Armstrong uses the example of planning a vacation. In this situation, money gives us the following benefits:

- Freedom of maneuver

- Options about where to stay

- Flexibility about what we can eat and do for leisure

Meanwhile, the virtues needed for a good vacation are:

• A sense of purpose

• Self-knowledge

• Canniness

• Resilience

• Spirit of adventure

• Cultural sensitivity

If we have money, but lack these virtues, we might end up with: "superficial entertainment, lackluster memories, shallow, inauthentic cultural experiences, self-denial and dissatisfaction." If we have these virtues but lack money, it's unlikely that we'll be able to take our vacation at all! Money helps multipotentialites pursue our passions, whether that means buying a camera to indulge in our new love of photography, enrolling in a rock climbing class, or funding a business.[2] Yet, without creativity, curiosity, and other such "virtues," money won't get us far. It's essential, but insufficient.

Differences in Financial Goals

Although we all need a certain amount of money to live, the amount required varies dramatically from person to person. Some people are frugal or minimalist by nature and care very

---

2. To make the multipotentialite lifestyle more affordable, I recommend borrowing equipment and supplies, or trading/bartering whenever possible, at least until you know that a particular interest is likely to stick. You can sell your supplies if you move on.

little about acquiring material goods. A level of income that meets their basic needs is enough for them to feel satisfied. Others care deeply about comfort or prestige and desire a very high income. Most of us fall somewhere in the middle, and we tend to care more about certain types of goods or services than others. An avid runner, for example, might spend a great deal of money on high-quality shoes, but very little dining at restaurants, because eating out is of less importance to them. In addition to our passions and preferences, we each have different obligations and expenses. We might be supporting children or other family members. We might live in a big, expensive city. We might lack health care or have heaps of student debt. Whatever your financial circumstances, it's important to get specific about what you value as well as your income goals. Simply seeking "more," without defining how much you need and why, will contribute to a chronic sense of never having enough.

What Are Your Financial Goals?

Here are four questions to ask yourself to help you get a better sense of your financial goals:

1. What is your basic survival budget (rent, bills, food, etc.) and what additional expenses do you have?

2. What do you value? Are there categories of goods or services that bring you great joy, and others that matter far less to you? This is personal and subjective, so try not to judge yourself. If you love

drinking lattes in the morning, that is completely fine! Maybe you don't care all that much about television and would hardly notice if you canceled your cable. Be honest about what you value and what you could live without. Knowing this will help you cut unnecessary costs and allocate more funds to the things that enhance your life.

3. What items or experiences would you need to have in your life to allow you to flourish? Let yourself dream a little here. What would your life look and feel like if you were to obtain these by reaching your financial goals?

4. What are your safety nets? Do you have friends or family members who would let you crash on their couch or lend you money if you were in a desperate situation?

Meeting Your Survival Needs First

It can take time and experimentation to build a career that supports your multipotentiality. You probably won't reach your income goals instantly, so it is wise to ensure that your basic survival needs are being met. This might mean temporarily finding or staying at a job that is less than ideal, relying on a marketable skill that doesn't completely light you up, living off savings, or reducing your living expenses by cutting costs, living with roommates, and so on.

When Tim Manley made the decision to become a professional artist and writer, he didn't quit his day job as a high school English teacher. He continued to teach and pursue his art on the side for a few years. When he felt as though he was nearly ready to leave, he decided that instead of quitting, he would take a year off to see whether he could sustain a creative practice full-time. He reduced his expenses by moving back in with his family and spent the year doing the sort of work he had been yearning to do. After that year, Tim returned to his teaching position and taught for one final school year, while saving up and getting the pieces in place for his transition. It was only after thinking long and hard about venturing off on his own, testing it out, reducing his expenses by leaning on family, and of course honoring his commitments by finishing out his contract that Tim made the jump. Sticking with a job that isn't our absolute ideal, but that pays the bills, may not sound glamorous. But it can be the (temporary) thing that makes our dreams possible. Having a reliable source of income makes it easier to experiment freely because it removes the pressure of needing our passions to generate income NOW!

Key Points About Money

- We need money to live and flourish, but the amount varies dramatically from person to person.

- Money is just one ingredient in a happy life.

- It's important to take note of our financial needs, goals, values, and circumstances when designing our lives.

- It can take time and experimentation to build a career that supports our multipotentiality. In the meantime, we should make sure that our basic survival needs are being met.

2. MEANING

For the happy and successful multipotentialites I spoke with, making a good income is not enough. They also need to feel like they are doing something that matters. In your case, our goal isn't to pay the bills by finding you a bunch of odd jobs that you couldn't care less about. Supporting yourself is important (as is variety—more on that in a moment), but none of that matters without a deeper sense that you're doing something meaningful.

We know an activity or project is meaningful by the way we feel while doing it. When asked how she defines meaning, Melea Seward, a self-described "communications and strategy consultant, speaker, improvisational storyteller and educator," described the sensation of her heart quickening and her breath becoming heavier: "You know it when you feel it. And you also know when you don't have it in your life. Without meaning, your world feels tiny and your life is routine." Engaging in a meaningful activity makes us feel as though we've stumbled upon something brilliant. We feel like we're tapping into a unique and special ability within ourselves or even channeling a creative force that is bigger than us. We may find that it is easy to get into a flow, where time has a tendency to slow down or speed up. A meaningful activity makes us feel energized or joyful. It can also be difficult and exhausting at times (just talk to a social worker—or a writer—and you'll see what I mean). When the work itself is difficult, we rely on a deeper sense that we're doing something important to carry us through.

The Importance of Asking Why

A powerful way to figure out what you find meaningful is to ask yourself a simple question: "Why?" Simon Sinek popularized this particular sense of the word *Why* in his influential TED talk "How Great Leaders Inspire Action." He argues that the brands and leaders that we are drawn to have a strong understanding of why they do what they do, and they feature that Why front and center. We can do the same in our lives by identifying our own personal Whys—the driving forces behind our passions.

The better we know ourselves and the forces that drive us, the easier it is to make career decisions that don't just satisfy our financial goals, but also *feel right*. We need to understand not just *what* has brought us a sense of meaning before (public speaking, accounting, research, illustration, counseling, etc.), but *why* these activities felt so fulfilling (because we got to inspire people, solve problems, learn new things, descend into a meditative state, help people feel seen, etc.). While working with children with developmental disabilities, Heather Matinde discovered that she loves helping people tap into the natural, tactile world so that they can feel better physically and emotionally. Knowing this about herself is what led her to start a minimalist sandal business. Minimalist (or barefoot) footwear has very little padding and no heel, so the wearer can feel the terrain beneath their feet. Many people report feeling free or unrestricted when wearing minimalist shoes. While different from her work with disabled children, this is another way in which Heather can help people sense nature in a tactile way, so that they can feel comfortable and empowered. In this way, this project is perfectly in line with Heather's Why.

Knowing our Whys can help us create a narrative around seemingly disparate interests and provide a starting point to consider new career options. For instance, if we know that one of our Whys is *simplifying complex ideas,* then we might find a sense of meaning through teaching, illustration, and working in a field like science communication.[3] If one of our Whys is *helping people feel safe,* we might find a sense of meaning in psychotherapy, personal training, social work, and even insurance! Only by experimenting can we know whether a field or profession will give us this sense of meaning, but knowing our Whys can give us clues as to where to begin experimenting in the first place.

What Are Some of Your Whys?

These exercises will help you figure out some of your Whys:

1. Think back to a time when you felt totally alive, lit up, and in your element. What were you doing? Close your eyes and try to remember what your surroundings were like, who was there, and how you felt. The more detail you can recall, the better. Maybe you'd even like to draw a picture. This moment can come out of your professional history or it can be very personal. When I first did this exercise, the image that popped into my head was making art and having tea parties with my stuffed animals at our round, wooden kitchen table as a kid. I used to lose hours at that table.

3. This is not an exclusive list.

2. Once you identify the specific activity (reading a book about history, pitching a marketing strategy, building furniture, writing a novel, designing a surgical robot with a team of mechanical engineers), zoom out. What was it *about* this activity that you loved? Why were you drawn to it? In my case, what I loved about my time at the kitchen table wasn't the specific medium of art or tea. It was the act of imagination and concoction. The kitchen table was a place I went to bring my ideas to life. It didn't matter if my ideas came out as paintings, homemade playdough, or story lines enacted by my toys. To this day, I continue to seek out, and be drawn to, work that involves *imagination* and *concoction.* It doesn't matter if this work takes the form of filmmaking, writing, or launching online communities. Each medium is just a different vehicle for imagination and concoction.

3. Repeat steps one and two for three to five other moments that made you feel alive. It's okay if your moments are very different from one another, and you were drawn to them for different or conflicting reasons.

4. On a new page or in a separate area, make a list of the Whys you uncovered.

5. Go back over each moment on your original list. Can you think of any other experiences you've had in your professional or private life that appealed to you for the same reasons?

6. Are there any other similarities between your moments? Did they involve other people? If so, what were these people like? Did your moments take place in quiet environments, or was there a lot of fast-paced energy around? Again, don't worry if the environments

seem to conflict. It's okay if you like both solitary and group activities. As multipotentialites, we want to expect and plan for our contradictions.

It's Okay to Have More Than One Why

It is tempting to try to whittle down all our interests and backgrounds into a single motivating force. The danger of trying to devise a single Why is the risk of oversimplifying things and just applying a new version of the specialist ideal to our lives. Understand the patterns and forces that move you, but learn to be comfortable with your plurality. You are a complex and nuanced creature. You contain contradictions and surprises. That's a good thing.

Having Enough Overall Money and Meaning

It would be fantastic if everything we're into produced income and felt deeply meaningful. We want to aim for as much overlap between meaning and profitability as possible, but multipotentialites are ever-changing creatures with many, many loves, and there is no shame in doing something purely for fun (or even purely for money).

It's easy to devalue interests that don't produce income, but be careful not to confuse profitability with value. An activity can be deeply valuable on a personal level, even if it isn't tied to our careers. It might provide us with opportunities to grow, to give back, to improve our mental or physical health, to spend quality time with our family, or with any number of other nonquantifiable but important benefits. Multipotentialites typically have an array of projects and activities in our lives, some of which are profitable and some of which aren't. Ultimately, it doesn't matter which of our pursuits bring in income as long as we have enough money to support ourselves, overall.

Similarly, it's okay to do something just for money.[4] We certainly shouldn't hate what we do, and different people have different tolerance levels for work that doesn't feed the soul, but it's okay to make use of a skill because it pays the bills. Neil Hughes is a freelance programmer. He is also a writer, stand-up comic, and mental health advocate. Most of his income comes from his programming work, which he enjoys well enough. Programming is his most lucrative skill, and even though it doesn't provide him with the same degree of meaning as his other projects, it is the thing that makes those projects possible. Like with money, what's important isn't that *everything* we do provide us with a sense of meaning, but that *overall,* we have enough meaning in our lives to feel like we are making a positive impact in the world.

Key Points About Meaning

- Multipotentialites need a sense of meaning in our lives to be happy.

- There's no official rule about whether or not an activity is meaningful, but we usually know it when we feel it.

- One way to identify the activities that bring us a sense of meaning is to figure out our Whys—the forces that motivate and move us.

4. This might be considered either a blasphemous or blatantly obvious statement, depending on who you ask.

- To figure out our Whys, we need to think about our past pursuits that gave us a sense of meaning. We should ask, not *what* these activities were, but *why* we enjoyed them. What was it that drew us in and made us feel alive?

- It's okay to have more than one Why and for our Whys to seem contradictory.

- There is nothing wrong with doing something purely for fun or even purely for money, as long as we have the money and meaning that we need in our lives, overall.

3. VARIETY

You've probably heard the saying, "Find something you love to do and you'll never have to work a day in your life." This advice is rather useless for multipotentialites, who by our nature, require variety to be happy. Even when we find something we love, we would be quite unfulfilled if we had to do it every day, forever. However, mainstream career advice doesn't typically recognize that variety is essential for some of us. It's rare to find a career counselor who will be on board with helping you launch a career in two (or more) very different fields at once. Most career books aim to help you whittle down your choices to a single, "perfect" fit, instead of helping you come up with a multifaceted profession that combines your interests and lets you wear multiple hats. The need for variety is rarely acknowledged, let alone prioritized.

When we have ample variation in our career, we go about our day doing activities that provide us with some combination of money and meaning, and we switch between projects at a frequency that feels right. All multipotentialites need variety in our lives to be happy, but as with money and meaning, the amount required is different from person to person. Too little variety makes us feel bored, frustrated, and upset that we aren't able to express the breadth of who we are. With too much variety, we become overwhelmed and frustrated because we aren't making as much progress as we would like.

Multipotentialites often invite too much variety into our lives by overbooking ourselves. We have an intense desire to learn and experience new things. We want to say yes to the YA novel idea we just came up with, the bike tour across Ireland we dream of taking, *and* to that insanely cool nautical archaeology graduate program we just discovered. We may very well be able to pursue all these things (and more) over the course of our life, but pursuing them all at once could overwhelm us to the point where we aren't having much fun.

Multipotentialites don't need to relegate ourselves to a single focus, but having too much on our plate can stress us out! Thankfully, there is a middle ground between doing just one thing and doing everything under the sun. Your job is to figure out the perimeter of your middle ground. It's different for everyone. Do you enjoy having three projects on your plate, but begin to feel overwhelmed when you add a fourth? Is that number much higher? Maybe you thrive with nine or ten projects on your plate. Or maybe you are at the sequential end of the spectrum that we discussed in Chapter 1 and really like to go deep in a single area before switching to the next.

The amount of variety we need doesn't just vary from person to person; it fluctuates over the course of each person's life. When I was studying filmmaking, I thought of little else. My film projects had a tendency to take over my life, and I would spend eight months of the year submerged in the production of a single twelve-minute film. There have been other times in my life when I've been involved in three or four different domains at once. At one point in my twenties, I was running a business, writing an album, taking a chemistry class, and volunteering as an after-school tutor. As I write this, I am currently involved in a multitude of business activities, including running an online community, preparing for a speaking engagement, and of course, writing this book. We go through different seasons. Sometimes it makes sense to dive deep into a single area, and other times a great deal of diversity energizes and excites us.

Variety Can Be Between Jobs or Within a Single Job

It's worth noting that filmmaking is an extremely interdisciplinary field. In other words, filmmakers use multiple skill sets every day: writing, drawing/storyboarding, directing, photography, editing, music composition, business, event planning, marketing, and more. I used to write, direct, produce, and score my films. I loved that I got to do so much! *And* it was easy to spend eight months thinking of little else.

If we're involved in an interdisciplinary field, we need fewer additional activities to satisfy our multipotentialite need for variety. A field like artificial intelligence, for example, blends psychology, philosophy, technology, neuroscience, computer science, mathematics, robotics, pattern recognition, machine learning, and visual perception. And sustainable development, as a field, requires an understanding of organizational development, economics, social justice, ecology, politics, technology, business, architecture, and culture. Projects in these fields may look, to an outsider, like "one thing," but they can provide us with heaps of variety. The more interdisciplinary a field is, the less variety we require. The opposite is also true.

How Much Variety Do You Need?

Here are some questions that will help you figure out how much variety you need in your life. The first three questions will help you understand your general patterns, and numbers 4 to 6 will help you assess your current situation.

1. Think of a time in your life when you felt bored or uninspired because you were doing too much of the same thing. How many projects were you working on? Were these projects interdisciplinary or fairly specialized?

2. Think of a time in your life when you felt completely overwhelmed by having too many different projects on your plate. How many projects were you working on? Were they interdisciplinary, or fairly specialized?

3. Think of a time in your life when you felt like you had the perfect balance of projects on your plate. How many projects were you working on? Were they interdisciplinary, or fairly specialized?

4. Think about your current mix of personal and professional projects and place an *X* on this line in the spot where you believe yourself to be:

Many, many projects ← → Currently just one thing

5. Now place an *X* in the spot on the line where you would *like* to be. (Note: This exercise may yield different results at different times in your life.)

6. Is the second *X* in a different spot from the first? What would it take for you to get there? What projects or activities could you cut from or add to your life?

The Importance of Experimenting

Although it's helpful to have a sense of how much variety you need in your life, it can be difficult to predict how much you will need in every new situation. Since the amount of variety we need fluctuates and depends on the nature of our individual projects, it's important to experiment and reflect (do you feel bored, overwhelmed, etc.?). Then you can add or subtract projects until you get closer to an amount that feels satisfying.

Key Points About Variety

• Career advice doesn't typically recognize the need for variety, although it is an absolute requirement for multipotentialites.

• Having enough variety means switching between different skills and projects at a frequency that feels right.

• The amount of variety we require is different for everyone and fluctuates over the course of our lives.

- The more interdisciplinary a project or field is, the fewer additional activities multipotentialites require to satisfy our need for variety.

- Experimentation is key. Pay attention to how you feel, and then add or subtract projects until you get the amount of variety that works for you.

DEFINING THE BIG PICTURE

Since this process is about designing a life, not just a career, it's important to take a step back and ask not simply what our ideal job or career is, but what our ideal *life* looks like. Only once we have an idea of what we're aiming for on a grander scale can we begin to figure out how to make that life work financially. Let's get a sense of your broader goals and how your career might fit into the overall puzzle.

What Would Your "Perfect Day" Look Like?

The Perfect Day exercise is a classic. It can give you clues about which direction to move in. It's also a powerful tool to help motivate you when you are in the thick of inertia, and need some inspiration.

1. Picture yourself waking up in the morning. What do your surroundings look like? Who's there? What do you do when you

get up? What do you do next? Keep describing your day until the moment you close your eyes at night.

2. How do you feel throughout the day? Do this exercise in the present tense and really try to put yourself in the shoes of this future you.

3. How does your Perfect Day match up with some of the Whys that you uncovered earlier?

I used to have trouble with this exercise because I could easily imagine multiple Perfect Days—different lives I'd like to try out. If this is a problem for you, try to be less specific about the activities in your day. Instead of imagining yourself pitching story lines for a medical drama in a writer's room, imagine a chunk of time during which you "pitch ideas and brainstorm with a team." That way you can swap in whatever group-oriented creative project you happen to be working on. You can even insert your Whys in these slots. Another option is to imagine multiple Perfect Days. If you have one Perfect Day in which you are an artist living in New York City and another in which you own a restaurant in a charming Spanish villa, describe them both. Pull out your Perfect Day and read through it (or add to it) whenever you need a reminder of what you're building and moving toward.

HOW MULTIPOTENTIALITES GET THE MONEY, MEANING, AND VARIETY WE NEED INTO OUR LIVES

After completing the exercises in this chapter, you should have a better sense of what you're looking for financially, personally, and spiritually. Your goals will obviously change with time, and you should never feel locked in to any of your answers, but having a general idea of the kind of life you want to create is an important starting point. Put your answers to these exercises somewhere safe, because we'll be coming back to them throughout the next four chapters.

You can now move forward and begin to define the specifics of your work life. How exactly will you get the money, meaning, and variety that you require? What field(s) will you pursue professionally? Where will your current skills fit into the mix? What kind of organization(s) will you work for—or will you be self-employed? It's time to get specific and begin generating some career ideas that are compatible with your particular mash-up of skills and interests.

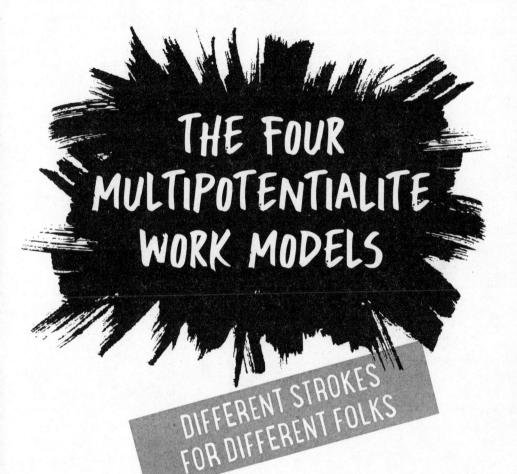

PART II

THE FOUR MULTIPOTENTIALITE WORK MODELS

DIFFERENT STROKES FOR DIFFERENT FOLKS

Although there isn't a single ideal career for multipotentialites, I've found that most happy multipotentialites use one of the following four work models.

WORK MODEL #1: THE GROUP HUG APPROACH

The Group Hug Approach is having one multifaceted job or business that allows you to wear many hats and shift between several domains at work.

Do you:

- Love multidimensional projects where you get to be involved in many different capacities?

- Want the "thing you do for money" to reflect the entirety of who you are (or close to it)?

- Feel overwhelmed when you have too many disconnected projects?

- Prefer to have a sense of synchronicity in your work so that anytime you're focusing on one area, that work contributes to a greater whole?

If you answered yes to two or more of these questions, pay extra close attention to the Group Hug work model, which we'll discuss in Chapter 4.

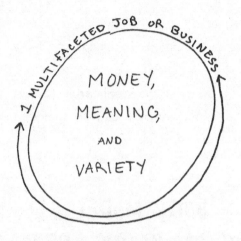

WORK MODEL #2: THE SLASH APPROACH

The Slash Approach is having two or more part-time jobs and/ or businesses that you flit between on a regular basis.

Do you:

- Like alternating frequently between very different subjects?

- Often find yourself fascinated by specialized or niche topics?

- Not care very much about combining your passions in service of a single entity?

- Value freedom and flexibility more than stability?

If you answered yes to two or more of these questions, you might just be a Slash careerist at heart. Chapter 5 will be your jam.

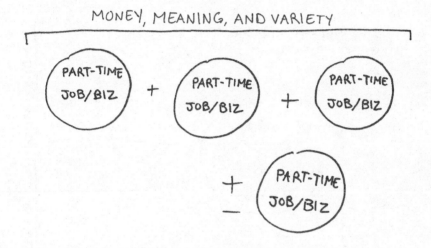

WORK MODEL #3: THE EINSTEIN APPROACH

The Einstein Approach is having one full-time job or business that fully supports you, while leaving you with enough time and energy to pursue your other passions on the side.

Do you:

- Value stability over flexibility?

- Want your paid work to be enjoyable, but don't feel as though it has to be the be-all and end-all?

- Find joy and meaning when you pursue your many fascinations for fun, as hobbies?

- Want to pursue something that doesn't usually come with a big paycheck?[1]

If you answered yes to two or more of these questions, check out the Einstein Approach in Chapter 6.

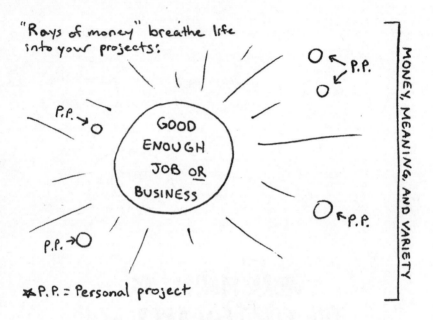

"Rays of money" breathe life into your projects:

P.P. → O

GOOD ENOUGH JOB OR BUSINESS

O ← P.P.
O ←

O ← P.P.

P.P. → O

✱P.P. = Personal project

MONEY, MEANING, AND VARIETY

WORK MODEL #4: THE PHOENIX APPROACH

The Phoenix Approach is working in a single industry for several months or years and then shifting gears and starting a new career in a new industry.

1. See: anything in the arts.

Do you:

- Become obsessed with things for fairly long periods of time?

- Find that months or years pass before you feel the itch to move on to a new area?

- Like going deep into particular subjects and often get mistaken for a specialist?

- Not require a ton of variety in your day to be happy?

If you answered yes to two or more of these questions, the phoenix might be your spirit animal. Learn all about the Phoenix Approach in Chapter 7.

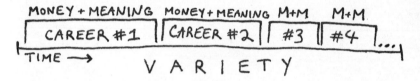

We'll be discussing each work model in depth in the next four chapters. We'll meet a lot of interesting multipotentialites along the way, and we'll consider what your life might look like if you were to adopt each framework.

IT'S OKAY TO MIX AND MATCH

The four work models described in this book provide plenty of opportunities for customization and flexibility. However, I wouldn't dare tell my multipotentialite readers to *choose one thing*! Mix and match the four approaches as you please. Switch models every few years. Be a hybrid. It's all good. These work models aren't meant to restrict you. They simply provide a structure and a starting place so that you can make sense of your many facets and conceptualize how they might translate into a fulfilling career and life.

THE GROUP HUG APPROACH

Imagine all your interests coming together in one giant group hug. This image might be hilarious, even shocking, but let's consider it metaphorically. What if finding or designing one career that brings together all your interests could be a reality? Surprise! **The Group Hug Approach is having one multifaceted job or business that allows you to wear many hats and shift between several domains at work.** Under the Group Hug Approach, you fulfill your needs for money, meaning, and variety within a single career. The cookie of your work has variety baked right into it, which allows your work to remain fresh and dynamic over time.

If you love multidimensional projects where you get to be involved in many different capacities and if you want the "thing you do for money" to reflect the entirety of who you are (or close to it), then a Group Hug career might just be what you're looking for.

SMOOSHING YOUR INTERESTS TOGETHER

A Group Hug career can be either *found* or *created*. You can seek out an interdisciplinary job that is compatible with your interests, or you can design a role or business that allows you to flex your different personality muscles and put all your selves to work. In either case, you are combining several subjects in one career via a highly scientific process I like to call "smooshing." *Smooshing is exactly what it sounds like—the blending together of disparate entities.* One might, for example, smoosh together interests in political science, cooking, anthropology, and education to create an organization that teaches children about different cultures through global cooking classes. Someone else might choose to become a musical therapist because it is a smoosh of their interests in music and psychology. Let's take a look at five strategies that multipotentialites use to smoosh their interests into dreamy Group Hug careers.

STRATEGY #1: WORKING IN A NATURALLY INTERDISCIPLINARY FIELD

Is there a field that happens to overlap with your interests? Working in an interdisciplinary field requires you to have an understanding of different industries and perspectives.[1] If they find the right fit, even the most variety-craving multipotential-ites can be at home in a single field.

Jimena Veloz is an urban planner, which is a career in a naturally interdisciplinary field. Over the course of a single week, you might find her: researching, mapping, conducting field visits, interviewing people, working with communities, drafting reports, organizing events, planning the implementation of policy, designing, communicating to the public, advocating for a project to be approved, and evaluating completed projects. She has ample opportunity to be both theoretical and practical. Jimena also gets to work in a variety of contexts:

> You can stay inside, do research, think nonstop and discuss with colleagues. But then you get to go out and do fieldwork. And the definition of "urban" is so broad that you can explore a number of different areas: housing, transportation, environment, education, arts, agriculture, economics, architecture, design, landscape, politics, history.

Fun fact: there are *so many* trained architects in the multipotentialite community. When I first spotted this pattern, I was surprised, but the more I think about it, the more sense it makes. Architecture is another naturally interdisciplinary field. It melds the arts and sciences to make magic ranging from tiny houses to the Golden Gate Bridge. Of course, there is a nearly unlimited number of interdisciplinary fields. Here are some: artificial intelligence, art therapy, integrative medicine, environmental

---

1. We looked at interdisciplinary fields (and my affinity for filmmaking) in Chapter 3 when we discussed the need for variety.

policy, robotics, video game design, bioethics, and counseling. Multipotentialites tend to be drawn to, and thrive in, fields like these.[2]

STRATEGY #2: WHERE DO THE MULTIPOTENTIALITES HANG OUT?

Have you ever felt a spark of interest in some field or another, only to realize that you'd probably be totally bored with it within a few months? Sometimes, a field that doesn't seem particularly multipotentialite friendly has a hidden sweet spot just for us. If you do a bit of digging, you might find an interdisciplinary specialty that variety seekers and the multitalented gravitate toward. Katy Mould studied medicinal chemistry in university. As she was approaching graduation, she found herself struggling to narrow in on a specialty. Most of her colleagues were specializing, but the idea of committing to one aspect of science felt limiting to her. Luckily, Katy discovered science communication, a subset within science that involves communicating scientific ideas to nonexperts. In her words,

> People who work in science communication need a broad but nuanced understanding of all aspects of

2. For a longer list of interdisciplinary fields, check out Appendix B.

science in order to tailor how they talk to different demographics about the same topic, but at a level matched to that audience's current understanding. They need strong skills in public speaking/performance, audience management, an understanding of different learning styles, creative flair, and the ability to convey information with passion often with little-to-no practice (i.e., the ability to "wing it"). The science communication world has a wonderful tendency to favor projects that are multidisciplinary. We help people grasp scientific concepts through unexpected, relatable contexts and, as such, the people drawn to work in the field tend to have multiple, varied interests and influences. I have been involved in projects combining arts/science, music/science, French/drama/science, programming/science, and food/science.

What appears to be a niche within the discipline of science is actually a multifaceted haven for multipotentialites. These occur more frequently than you might think, which is one reason that we often fail to recognize multipotentialites when we look around at the people in our lives. If you're pursuing a field that doesn't feel smooshy enough (a.k.a. might kill you with lack of variety), you might just need to do a little research. Maybe there's a specialty or school of thought within the field that will totally resonate with your eclectic nature.

Education is a broad discipline and teachers must take on many roles each day. They constantly shift from counselor to facilitator to leader. They need to be able to cater to different learning styles, negotiate cultural differences, and handle their students' social or emotional issues. Effectively running a classroom is like running a tiny country—it's remarkable!

Some people find that being a teacher, in and of itself, provides them with sufficient variety. Others just need more. Sara Meister is an elementary school teacher at a Waldorf school. The Waldorf approach is a unique educational methodology, based on the teachings of Austrian philosopher Rudolf Steiner. When asked what a typical school day looks like in her elementary school classroom, Sara explains,

> The main curricular piece of the day is called Main Lesson. This is a two-hour block of study first thing, Monday to Friday. It begins with a Morning Circle— movement, games, verses, songs, recorder playing, alliteration, bean bag toss, modeling, figure drawing, mental math, spelling, you name it. Then the previous day's lesson is reviewed orally or via an activity. Then a story is told with the new day's content. Lastly, the children work with the previous day's lesson or this day's lesson in a creative way. This may look like a group authoring a play, painting a picture, writing a summary, or modeling a map of Africa from clay. The emphasis is on hands-on and exploratory learning. The teacher is "the world"—they bring the world to the students through the lessons they teach. They emphasize truth, beauty, and goodness. (Critical thinking begins in middle school classrooms.)

Throughout grade school, a Waldorf instructor teaches almost every subject to a single class. This gives them an opportunity to draw analogies between the material in different subjects. At a traditional Western school, disciplines are kept separate and conceptualized as distinct.[3] A student in a typical American school might go to English class, move on forty-five minutes later to science class, then proceed to physical education, and so on. Teachers in these schools rarely collaborate or draw connections between subjects. Waldorf teachers move through the day with their students, but they also move up the grades with their class. A teacher begins teaching first grade, and when their class moves on to second grade, they teach them their second-grade material. The following year, the teacher works with the same group of students on third-grade material, and so on, until the class finishes eighth grade.

Sara chose to become a Waldorf teacher for many reasons, but enjoying a great deal of variety and creativity in her work is certainly a key perk. She is encouraged to integrate the things she's passionate about into her teaching, and she is able to shift between forms more freely than she would at a conventional elementary school. Since she teaches many subjects to a single group of students, Sara can illustrate the connections between seemingly disparate ideas. Because Sara teaches her students a multitude of subjects over the span of eight years, she doesn't have to rehash the same material year after year. Her work continues to be fresh and engaging. Seeking out interdisciplinary sweet spots like Sara's is one of the many multipotentialite ninja career moves. Sometimes you just need to find your people.

3. Fun fact: In Finland, they have just reformed the education system to replace subject-based teaching with an interdisciplinary curriculum model!

STRATEGY #3: WORKING FOR AN OPEN-MINDED ORGANIZATION

Another way to establish a Group Hug career is finding a forward-thinking employer who values your ideas and wants to make use of your strengths. Although most job listings are still rather specialized (which can be disheartening for a multipotentialite), an exciting shift is happening. More and more companies are waking up to the value of talented generalists. This is partly due to the changing landscape of business; small organizations and start-ups tend to be more open-minded than large organizations, both in ideology and in structure. An employee is less likely to hear "that's not how we do things," at a small company. Start-ups often rely on people who can take on a variety of responsibilities because they don't have the budget or infrastructure to hire a separate person for every little role. Of course, this isn't true of all start-ups, and there are plenty of larger companies seeking creative minds to help them stay at the forefront of the changing economy.

Want to know if a company is multipotentialite friendly? You can often get a sense by looking at their marketing material and projects, researching the CEO, or even looking at the language of the job listing itself. Threadless is a popular online apparel shop. Artists from around the world submit designs, and the community votes for its favorites. The winning designs are printed onto T-shirts, tanks, and hoodies and sold through the site. Threadless is known for its playful ethos and its help-wanted ads scream multipotentialite-wanted. Here are some qualities they were looking for in a recent job listing for a creative director:

About you:

- Manage and motivate a cross-disciplined team of designers, production artists, photographers, videographers, and copywriters

- Contribute to product strategy and vision (not just "how it should look/work" but "what we should build and why")

- Work closely with our product, community, marketing, digital, and partnerships teams to oversee the user experience of a product from idea to launch (and beyond)

- Willing to embrace stepping outside of your comfort zone and learning new things from designing a trade show booth experience to creating building signage to making a video spot on the scrap

- Strong organization skills with an ability to juggle multiple projects and timelines

Don't you just want to start working for them right now? The job description makes it clear they are looking for someone who can work with big teams in different departments, step outside their comfort zone, take on challenges, learn new skills, and juggle multiple projects. They even throw in words like *cross-disciplined* and express a desire to hear your ideas and input about the direction of the company. Simply put, there is no way a specialist would be able to fill this role.[4]

4. Sorry to report that the position is no longer available. I was tempted to apply myself!

STRATEGY #4: MAKING AN EXISTING JOB MORE PLURAL

Yes, it's wonderful to get hired at an organization that recognizes and values your diverse talents. But what should you do if you already *have* a job, with a company that doesn't seem to care about your many skills? Not all employers will be open to you stepping outside of your job description. However, some of them can be convinced, provided you approach the issue in the right way.

Multipotentialites often use one particular skill set to get in the door at a company. Once they've been working at their job for a while and have proven themselves, they persuade their employers to let them assume more responsibility and change focuses within the company. Digital media artist Margaux Yiu was originally hired to compile multimedia presentations. But over the course of the fifteen years she's been with her company, she has assumed a number of other roles at work. She's managed their website, led the front-end design team, acted as head photographer and videographer, trained coworkers in media processes, and filled in for other positions such as video editor and content manager. How has she gotten the golden ticket to do so many different things over the years? She pays attention to gaps in the business—things that they are neglecting or doing poorly—and she proposes solutions. When she wanted to be put in charge of web development, Margaux explained to her boss how important a strong web presence would be (this was back in the nineties). When she became head videographer, it was because her company had begun shooting footage for their website. Given her background in photography, and the lack of experience her colleagues had in this area, Margaux was able to swoop in and lead the team, as well as train her colleagues in basic lighting and camera techniques.

The best way to get permission to smoosh your other interests into your work is to **emphasize the value that you will provide to the company.** Instead of pitching your array of wonderful abilities, lead with how this particular project will benefit them. Paint them a picture of the awesome end result you'll serve up. (And, hey, if you *must* use your writing/math/animation/tap-dancing skills to get that result, so be it!) When approaching her employer, Margaux did not say "I'm really interested in learning HTML. Aaaand I have a background in photography. Oh, I also really love video editing, can I be in charge of that?" Rather, she explained just how important it was to their bottom line for them to have a nice website and professional-looking videos.

Jesse Waldman was hired at a small plant nursery to work in the retail shop. After working there for a few weeks, he approached the owner and showed her how they could sell their merchandise online, using skills he had acquired from an outside interest in e-commerce. Jesse was immediately put in charge of developing the company's online shop (and given a raise). Like Margaux, Jesse didn't just casually mention that he happens to know a lot about online shopping carts. Instead, he explained what an impact an online shop would make on profits and how easy it would be to set up and maintain.

If you would like to integrate particular skills into your work, try coming up with some initiatives that will allow you to use these skills while helping the company grow or run more smoothly. When you pitch your project, emphasize the latter. Frame it in terms of *their* interests. What do they care about? How will this project bring value to the company?

STRATEGY #5: STARTING A BUSINESS

The easiest way to work for a boss who lets you wear many hats at work is to be your own boss. There are few careers more multifaceted than entrepreneurship. Running a business means product development, marketing, sales, psychology, branding, customer relations, internal structures, law, and finance. You don't need to be an expert in each of these areas to start a business (most of us figure them out as we go), but you *do* need to possess an intense drive to learn, experiment, and do a bit (or a lot) of everything, particularly at the beginning.

When I was growing up, no one ever told me that starting a business was a thing. I didn't even know what an entrepreneur was until I was well into my twenties. I probably assumed it meant some business guy in a suit, and, as a depressed teenager with a propensity for punk rock and introspection, I had no interest in such things. I certainly didn't consider myself an entrepreneur when I started booking shows for my band or building websites for my artist friends for a few hundred bucks a pop (or sometimes for a hug and some chocolate chip cookies). But that's exactly what I was.

Don't let the word *entrepreneur* turn you off. There are many different types of businesses, ranging from large-scale investor-funded ones (like you might see on the television show *Shark Tank*), to the family-run Indian restaurant down the street, to the online collective selling radical zines, tarot readings, and homemade soaps. By the end of this chapter, you'll have an idea of what's possible for multipotentialite entrepreneurs. And you'll want to start a business. Or five.

The Renaissance Business

So, entrepreneurship can seem like *the* solution. But there is a particular snag for multipotentialites. In the same way that a broad field may not be interdisciplinary enough for a particular individual, entrepreneurship, although it has many angles, may still feel straight and narrow. This can be extra true if your business is highly niched. You might love cooking, but find yourself becoming bored after a few years of running a catering business. You might be a great social media manager, but become frustrated and want to explore new things after working with clients on their campaigns day in and day out. Thankfully, there is a broader type of business—one that allows you to shift between subjects on a regular basis. I call this the Renaissance Business, and it is, perhaps, best understood through example.

Mark Powers isn't your typical drummer. Instead of deriving his income from some combination of performing and teaching, as many professional musicians do, Mark smooshed a few of his other passions into the mix: technology, anthropology, philanthropy, speaking, and travel. The resulting business gives Mark numerous outlets for his creativity (and numerous revenue streams). Mark teaches percussion, not only in person, but online, using Skype. Because the reach of his business extends beyond his physical location, he is able to work with students from all over the world. In 2011, Mark flew to Uganda to record youth choirs and local village musicians. He sells the resulting album, *Amaloboozi* (which means "voices" in the Luganda language), through his website and sends proceeds to organizations doing humanitarian work in those regions.

Because one-on-one teaching and international philanthropy aren't enough, Mark also creates and sells digital guides for percussionists and teachers. He spends a lot of time writing, and he recently released a children's book called *I Want to Be a Drummer!* Mark runs workshops at schools and community centers and in corporate settings and has hosted TEDx events. Of course, he still performs live with various musicians, too. While a non-multipotentialite might find this lifestyle overwhelming, Mark loves it. His Renaissance Business allows him to lead a rich, dynamic life in which he gets paid to be his true, full self.

Marketing for Hippies provides marketing training for conscientious, green, and holistic small businesses, and it's another A+ example of a Renaissance Business. Tad Hargrave dreamed up this gem by mixing two of his fascinations: activism and marketing. Look at Tad's biography and try to tell me that this isn't the ideal Group Hug for him:

> Tad Hargrave is a hippy who developed a knack for marketing (and then learned how to be a hippy again). Despite years in the non-profit and activist world, he finally had to admit he was a marketing nerd and, in the end, he became a marketing coach for hippies. Maybe it was because he couldn't stand seeing his hippy friends struggle to promote their amazing, green and holistic

projects. Maybe it was because he couldn't keep a 9–5 job to save his life.

Tad is the perfect person to teach marketing to conscientious entrepreneurs, because he has backgrounds in both areas. He can translate marketing principles, which might not typically appeal to this audience, in a way that feels ethical and understandable to hippies. Not only does Tad's eclectic background make Marketing for Hippies possible, it allows him to stand out from the thousands of other businesses on the planet that provide marketing training.

Here are a few more examples of Renaissance Businesses:

- Pielab: a café and community space located in Greensboro, Alabama, that offers initiatives such as bike repairs and catering apprenticeships. Their tagline is *Pie + Conversation = Social Change.*

- Mothership HackerMoms: the first-ever women's hackerspace in the world. Located in Berkeley, California, they offer on-site child care as well as a space for parents to work, create, and collaborate.

- The Laundromat Café: a cozy café, Laundromat, and bookstore in Copenhagen, Denmark. Similar hybrid Laundromat-cafés have recently begun popping up around the United States.

- Meshu: a geographically inspired jewelry company. Customers place an order by submitting geographical locations that are meaningful to them. The Meshu team plots a path between the locations, creating a necklace, earrings, cuff links, or ring using the shape.

- Abe Cajudo: "Full Service Creative Human" (at abecajudo.com) helps businesses and brands stand out through high-impact multimedia storytelling. This can take the form of web development, graphic design, video production, Kickstarter consulting, or online course creation.

Renaissance Businesses are sometimes perceived as being very niche. But imagine the person who uses their backgrounds in personal finance, counseling, and LGBTQ rights to help same-sex couples manage their money. This highly specific offering involves an understanding of, and a shifting between, several realms and modes of thought. In its specificity, it contains multitudes.

I am often confronted with the misconception that smooshing several subjects together in one business will lead to a confusing and unfocused brand. But Renaissance Businesses can be extremely profitable *and* attract a rabid community/customer base by highlighting their unique philosophies. The key is to make the relationships between the subjects and offerings crystal clear. If you know how your business fits together, and you communicate it to your audience clearly, you are well on your way.

TO SMOOSH OR NOT TO SMOOSH, THAT IS THE QUESTION

Starting your own business does not require that you integrate every single one of your interests. Remember the goal here: you want an overall sense of variety in your *life*. That variety can be achieved internally—within one multifaceted job or business—or externally, by pairing together two or more disparate businesses, jobs, or hobbies. In the next chapter, you'll meet multipotentialite entrepreneurs who run multiple businesses. You decide whether to combine your passions or keep them separate. Both approaches can work. The decision is really a matter of personal preference.

EXPLORING YOUR INTERESTS OUTSIDE OF WORK

Although a Group Hug job is more interdisciplinary than a typical job, many multipotentialites still have hobbies outside of their work. Margaux volunteers as a tutor for high school students. She is a passionate photographer. When I spoke with her, she was fascinated with making and deconstructing pop-up books. When Sara isn't teaching or planning her lessons, she gardens, cooks, and practices yoga.

It's difficult to find one career that encompasses *all* your passions, but finding a job that allows you to explore *many* of them while getting paid is pretty sweet. You shouldn't, however, feel as though you need to fit absolutely everything into your paid work. As we've already discussed, there is nothing wrong with engaging with an interest or activity purely for fun, on your own time.

Trying on the Group Hug Approach

Now that we've explored the Group Hug Approach, let's see how your interests fit into this framework. It's time to generate some smooshy career ideas, so get out a pen and paper, and let's brainstorm!

CREATE YOUR MASTER LIST OF INTERESTS

Write down every interest, passion, skill, and curiosity, past and present, that you can think of. Do not censor yourself. It doesn't matter if you aren't currently involved in the activity, or if it's a very new or fleeting interest. When completing exercises like these, we have a tendency to discredit our accomplishments, so try to adhere to this rule: if at any point during this exercise, you wonder whether or not to include something, include it.

REFINE YOUR LIST

Cross out your "dead" interests—the items on your list that you have no desire to touch again anytime soon. Star the items on your list that sound especially exciting to you right now.

CREATE SUBGROUPS

Presumably, some of the interests on your master list fit together more naturally than others. On a new page, group these similar interests together and give them a name. For example, hiking, biking, and camping might be lumped together under "Outdoor Adventure." Photography, drawing, printmaking, and guitar, might fall under the heading of "Art" or "Creative Expression." International studies, travel, and activism might fall under "Politics" or "Social Justice." Don't worry about coming up with the perfect headings. Your group and subgroup names don't need to be perfect for this exercise to be helpful.

PAIR TOGETHER YOUR SUBGROUPS AND INDIVIDUAL INTERESTS

What would you find at the intersections of the various items and subgroups on your list? It's okay if your interests seem unrelated. Pair them together anyway, and see what kind of ingenious/hilarious career ideas you can come up with. Anthropological economics? Musical ecology? Why not?

ARE THERE ANY PREEXISTING FIELDS AT THESE INTERSECTIONS?

Research your pairs to see if there are any disciplines that exist at these intersections. Examples: Artificial intelligence, as previously mentioned, is a blend of psychology, philosophy, technology, neuroscience, computer science, mathematics, robotics, pattern recognition, machine learning, and visual perception. Filmmaking involves storytelling, writing, photography, design, music, planning, and so on. Bioethics is a field at the intersection of health, politics, law, and philosophy.

WHERE, WITHIN EACH FIELD, DO THE MULTIPOTENTIALITES HANG OUT?

For each of your subgroups, do some research and see whether there are any interdisciplinary specialties within the field. Example: functional clothing design is a branch of design that combines design, art, biology, chemistry, engineering, and social science. It involves making clothing that serves an additional purpose, anything from helping people with physical disabilities to keeping astronauts safe in space.

SEEK OUT FORWARD-THINKING COMPANIES

Do you know of any companies that have a reputation for treating their employees well and giving them a lot of freedom? Do some research and see what you come up with. Keep an eye out for words that call out to multipotentialites such as *creative, cross-disciplinary,* and *adaptable.*

GENERATE SOME RENAISSANCE BUSINESS IDEAS

What are some business ideas that would allow you to combine your interests? Examples: a coffee shop that doubles as a coworking space; a holistic health practice.

COULD YOU BRING KNOWLEDGE OR SKILLS FROM ONE INTEREST TO AN AUDIENCE RELATED TO A SECOND INTEREST OF YOURS?

You might be surprised to find that your skills in one area could be really helpful to a totally different group. Try filling in the blanks:

_____ FOR _____

    (INTEREST #1)   (AUDIENCE RELATED TO

                                    INTEREST #2)

I love the absurd pairings that come out of this exercise like "scuba diving for history buffs" or "improv classes for corporate teams." I love it even more because both of these services exist in real life. You'll probably come up with some pairings that wouldn't fly, but don't discredit a business idea right away, just for sounding a little unusual. Would your investing knowledge be helpful to nonprofits? Could you use your programming chops to build an online scheduling application for music teachers?

PUTTING IT TOGETHER

On a new sheet of paper, make a list of all the smooshy career and business ideas you've generated throughout these exercises.

CROSS-CHECK FOR MEANING, MONEY, AND VARIETY

Compare each of the career ideas you generated to your answers from the exercises in Chapter 3. For each career, ask:

- Is this career in line with one or more of my Whys?

- Is there an audience who would pay for the service that this career provides?

- Would this career provide me with enough (but not too much) variety?

- Is this career compatible with my Perfect Day?

Obviously, it is difficult to guess the salary of a particular job or the profitability of a business idea. And if a career doesn't seem to fit into the structure of your Perfect Day or align easily with your Whys, that doesn't mean that you should immediately disqualify it. You might be surprised by how right it feels in practice. And it's entirely possible that your notion of the Perfect Day may change.

Herein lies the friction between knowing thyself / planning on the one hand, and experiential wisdom on the other. There's only so much we can know from doing a theoretical exercise. You won't truly know whether a career is a good fit for you until you begin exploring it. If one or more of the careers on your list is really calling to you, that's enough of a reason to look into it further. But keep the above questions in mind as you experiment, and come back to them when you have more information and are in a better position to answer them accurately.

TAKING ACTION

If you're excited about pursuing a Group Hug career, decide on one to three small action steps that you can take this week to get started. These are personal, and they'll depend on your situation and the nature of your ideas, but here are a few possible examples:

- Contact someone who works in one of the interdisciplinary fields or specialties you identified to see if they'd be willing to answer some of your questions.

- Begin writing a cover letter for one of the multipotentialite-friendly companies you discovered.

- Research the market for one of your Renaissance Business ideas. Is there an audience for this product/service?

KEY POINTS FROM THIS CHAPTER

The Group Hug Approach allows you to get all your money, meaning, and variety needs met in a single career. Here are the key points we went over in this chapter:

- The Group Hug Approach is having one multifaceted job or business that allows you to wear many hats and shift between several domains at work.

- You can use several strategies to find or create a Group Hug career: you can work in a naturally interdisciplinary field, seek out a multifaceted niche within a field, work for a forward-thinking organization, be proactive and make a narrow job more plural, or start a business.

- Interdisciplinary fields like urban planning and artificial intelligence require an understanding of many disciplines and perspectives. Multipotentialites tend to be drawn to and thrive in fields like these.

- There are often interdisciplinary specialties within otherwise narrow fields that multipotentialites gravitate toward.

- Some organizations are composed of multipotentialites and actively seek out other generalists to join the team. Pay attention to the language of job listings and look for words like *creative, cross-disciplinary, adaptable,* and so on.

- Multipotentialites sometimes get in the door at a company by highlighting one skill set. After dazzling their employer with their great work, they convince them to let them assume additional responsibilities. They do this by emphasizing the value that their proposed project will bring to the company.

- Entrepreneurship is a natural fit for multipotentialites because there are many facets to running a business, from product development, to sales, marketing, design, and so on.

- But running a business doesn't always provide enough variety for multipotentialites, particularly if the business is highly niche. Some people therefore choose to create a Renaissance Business: one business within which multiple subjects are integrated.

THE SLASH APPROACH

Morgan Siem leads a triple life. Ten hours a week, she works at a nonprofit organization called the Human Kindness Foundation, where she sends meditation and mindfulness books to prisoners who request them. Two days a week, Morgan does freelance marketing, which she transitioned to after leaving a corporate job in the advertising industry a few years ago. Morgan is also an aerial silks artist and is occasionally hired for performances.[1] These three radically different revenue streams combine to make Morgan a nonprofit worker / freelance marketer / artist. See those slashes?

The Slash Approach, also known as a "portfolio career," is having two or more part-time jobs and/or businesses that you flit between on a regular basis. Unlike the Group Hug work model, where your passions are combined in a single endeavor, here

---

1. If you aren't familiar with aerial silks, imagine someone climbing, flipping, and spinning in giant hanging silk fabric!

they remain separate and distinct. You are the tour guide *slash* yoga teacher *slash* programmer *slash* textile artist, or the teacher *slash* lawyer *slash* choreographer. As a multipotential-ite using this work model, you'll typically have two to five work projects, each of which provides different levels of money and meaning so that the overall balance is right. You meet your need for variety not by working in an interdisciplinary field (though that sometimes happens as well), but by cycling through a few disparate domains.

A SLASH CAREERIST BY CHOICE

In Chapter 3, we talked about the importance of ensuring that your survival needs are being met while you build a career that is better aligned with your multipotentialite nature. Especially in light of the ways that economies are changing, both mul-tipotentialites and non-multipotentialites sometimes cobble together multiple part-time jobs to pay the bills. For most of them, this is a temporary measure on the road to figuring out a better-paying work scenario. But it can really look a lot like a Slash career!

Our goal here is not for you to build a career that simply keeps you afloat. Recall the three elements of a happy multi-potentialite life: money, variety, and *meaning*. A Slash career is, by definition, intentional. Of course, there will always be an element of financial necessity implicit in any career choice, but happy Slash careerists aren't forced into this structure out of necessity. As author and entrepreneur Penelope Trunk explains,

A portfolio career is not the same thing as holding down three bad jobs and wishing you could figure out what to do with yourself. Rather, it's a scheme you pursue purposefully and positively, as a way to achieve a mixture of financial and personal goals.

Many times we come to the Slash Approach through mental or emotional circumstances (not just for financial reasons). Morgan chose to embrace the Slash work model after nearly burning out at her full-time job. She had enjoyed her work in the past, but the long hours were beginning to take a toll on her health. Quitting her full-time position to embrace several part-time jobs, not only reduced her stress, it gave her a sense of purpose, freedom, and variety that she had been longing for.

SLASH CAREERISTS TEND TO BE EMPLOYED / SELF-EMPLOYED

As we explore the dynamic Slash Approach, you'll meet multipotentialites with multiple part-time jobs, multipotentialites who own a few different businesses, artists who work in more than one medium, and various combinations thereof. You'll notice that many Slashers[2] are both employed and self-employed—they mix up both their income structures and their work activities. For simplicity's sake, I've used the word *slash*

2. Don't be scared!

to refer to any kind of revenue stream, be it a job, a business, freelance work, or another project.[3]

IS THE SLASH APPROACH RIGHT FOR YOU?

Do you do your best work when you alternate frequently between different subjects? Do you have a mad passion for a specialized or niche topic but feel trapped by the very idea of committing to it full-time? Does the project of combining your passions or skills in service of a single entity[4] just not do it for you? If you answered *yes, heck yes,* or *hallelujah* to any of the above, there may be a Slash career in your future. This work model offers a ton of flexibility, which can be a blessing or a curse. It's a good option for those who are self-directed and have an independent or entrepreneurial spirit.

Remember back in Chapter 1, when we looked at the simultaneous–sequential spectrum? We know that some of us have the constitution for doing a million things all at once, and some of us like to focus on a smaller number of things at a time. Slash careerists have to balance and juggle different revenue streams in day-to-day life. So, if you found yourself closer to

3. Here's where I acknowledge the semantic inaccuracy of using the word *slash* in this way. I realize that the slash is the thing *between* two words, not the words themselves. However, it makes things so much simpler to refer to the revenue streams that compose a Slash career as *slashes*. And anyway, Marci Alboher did this first, in her great book *One Person / Multiple Careers*. So that's what we're going with. My apologies to the grammar nerds (including my wife). You're the best.

4. Such as a Group Hug job or Renaissance Business, which we looked at in Chapter 4.

the simultaneous end of the spectrum, then slashing might be a good fit. However, if you've figured out you're a die-hard sequential multipotentialite, it might just overwhelm you.

Part-Time Is the Dream

Working a few hours a week at different jobs or projects provides a fun, flexible, and variety-filled week. If you've ever had a typical, full-time job, you know this can be hard to come by in that world. Some multipotentialites feel that doing *anything* full-time just isn't an option. That's okay! When asked about her choice to have three part-time jobs, Morgan Siem expressed a sentiment that is common among Slash careerists: she enjoys each of her slashes a great deal but wouldn't want to be tied to any of them full-time. In her words,

> I love that all of my jobs are part-time because I don't want to give up any of them. My work at the Human Kindness Foundation, for example, is so important to me. And ten hours a week is the perfect amount.

Part-time work is sometimes considered inferior to full-time employment, but for Slash careerists, Part-Time + Part-Time + Part-Time ± Part-Time = The Dream.

Each Slash Fulfills a Different You

We're all multifaceted, folks—even specialists. If you choose to build a Slash career, each slash will allow you to use a different skill set and tap into a different part of your identity. Amy Ng is the creative lead at a PR firm two days a week. She teaches a class on creativity and entrepreneurship once a week at a local college. Her third slash is running her online community, Pikaland, where she blogs, leads workshops, and designs zines for an audience of artists and illustrators.[5] Amy's work at the PR agency provides her with the opportunity to collaborate with a team in a fast-paced environment. She likes being a college instructor because teaching gives her a sense of contribution, as well as a physical and social experience that she doesn't get sitting behind a computer screen. And Pikaland is an incredible outlet for Amy's creative and personal expression. It allows her to inspire people on a global scale and make use of her entrepreneurial and artistic skills. Each slash in a Slash career provides a different kind of experience, requires a unique skill set, and challenges you in a different way.

F*ck Boredom

Multipotentialites often naturally gravitate toward interdisciplinary fields. But sometimes, in a very upsetting Romeo-and-Juliet-type scenario, we find ourselves falling in love with a specialized subject. We may hope that this is our chance to delve professionally into a new area. We may see the economic potential in tapping into that niche market. Yet, hopefully we are self-aware enough to know that if we commit ourselves solely to something so narrow, we put ourselves at risk. We might burn out or—worse—*get bored*.

Theodore Jordan designed his career around several specialized offerings in order to confront this problem. His part-

5. At first glance, you might think that Amy's PR job is funding her other projects. It's not. In fact, when we spoke, she told me that she could live comfortably off her revenue at Pikaland.

time projects almost couldn't be any more "niche." Here are Theodore's slashes:

- *Sound and Soundware Designer:* Theodore creates sounds that are used as samples in music sequencers. He also makes soundtracks for paranormal/ghost-hunting TV shows. Listening to him describe this work, I think he sounds a bit like a mad scientist who is having all too much fun. I mean, "I recently froze a microphone in a puddle and recorded the sound of people skating over it"?! Yes, kids, you can make money this way.

- *Writer/Self-Publisher:* Using his expertise from the previous slash, Theodore wrote a book about running an indie soundware label. He's in the process of revising it and releasing a second edition.

- *Insurance-Related Website Designer:* He's a go-to guy for designing insurance company websites. He was working on three sites when we spoke and he loves using his creativity to make them just a little more interesting than industry standard.

- *Online Shopping Cart Blogger:* True story! Theodore describes himself as a "shopping cart nerd," and his e-commerce blog provides him with an outlet for his passion, as well as a revenue stream.

- *Guided Meditation Program Developer:* By designing and recording guided meditations for people to use on their phones and computers, Theodore has found a way to combine his interests in sound design and mindfulness.

Okay, so that's a lot of slashes![6] But it's not a coincidence that he has six slashes and that they all happen to be fairly specialized. The narrower our slashes are, the more of them we require to meet our need for variety. If we are interested in one interdisciplinary field, then a single job or business might satisfy our need for variety. But multipotentialites can and do thrive in narrow markets. It's just that we may need to be involved in *multiple* narrow markets to do our best work and stay engaged in the long run.

Freedom and Flexibility

I was once talking about Slash careers with a friend who lives in Los Angeles and she gave me a knowing look. "Oh, that's just how everyone makes a living here," she said. My friend was overgeneralizing, of course. There are plenty of people who live in L.A. and have regular day jobs. Her comment touches on two important things, though: (1) Slashing is a common way for artists like her to make a living and (2) There are a lot of aspiring artists in L.A. The flexibility of part-time work makes it easier to accommodate last-minute gigs, attend auditions, and say yes to creative projects. Not everyone using the Slash Approach is an artist, and not all artists use the Slash Approach, but there is a sweet, sweet overlap going on.

Another reason that artists are drawn to the Slash work model is that careers in the arts can take longer to establish than careers in other industries. Slashing allows artistically in-

6. On top of this, Theodore is a husband and father of two small children. When I asked him about his productivity strategies, he told me that he tries to wake up at 5 A.M. every day to get four hours of uninterrupted work in before his family wakes up. Remember when I told you that multipotentialites are the furthest thing from slackers?

clined multipotentialites to lean on other, more easily monetized interests while getting our artistic careers off the ground.

The Blessing and Curse of Self-Direction

To sustain a flourishing Slash career, we must be self-motivated and independent. We need to manage our own schedules. We have to be willing to veer from society's beaten path, but adhere to the standards and schedules we set for ourselves. If you're someone who is comfortable doing your own thing and organizing your time, then slashing could be a go for you. If, on the other hand, you thrive when being told what to do and when to do it, then you would probably prefer a different work model. It is common for Slash careerists to be averse to traditional employment and even to dislike authority.

MAKING THE JUMP TO A SLASH CAREER

There are three paths that lead multipotentialites toward Slash careers.

1. We Want Out of Our Full-Time Job

Some multipotentialites transition to a Slash career after working in a full-time position and realizing that we want more control over our work and our time. Our first slash is often a freelance version of a prior full-time job. We add additional slashes to our roster until we're good, in our wallets *and* our souls. Morgan made her transition when she left her advertising job and began doing freelance marketing work for a handful of clients. She used the connections she'd made in her previous job to find her first few clients, and flourished from there.

2. We Are Presented with a Part-Time Opportunity

When someone notices an aptitude and offers to pay us for a particular skill, it can launch us into a surprising or longed-for Slash career. This is how Bethel Nathan became an award-winning wedding officiant. Knowing she had a background in public speaking, her brother asked if she would officiate his wedding. Soon after, two close friends asked her to officiate their weddings. She loved it and received wonderful feedback from the guests. After careful consideration and research, Bethel began marrying couples professionally. A couple years later, she started two additional businesses: a consulting agency and a micropublishing company, rounding out her Slash career.

3. We Just Dive In and Refine as We Go

Some people begin Slash careers by taking on a hodgepodge of random jobs and then refining their work portfolio based on:

- which slashes they enjoy,

- which slashes are the most profitable, and

- which opportunities present themselves.

Andy Mort began his foray into slashing when his friends found themselves overwhelmed, caring for their newborn child:

My Slash career starting pretty much by accident, when friends of mine had a baby. One of them was a doctor and the other was studying to become a church minister, right alongside the full-time occupation of first-time parenting. They were struggling. They had no time to cook, to clean, to do the washing, and we were joking one day about how I could do meals on wheels for them. Before I knew it, I received an e-mail with the offer of eight hours work a week doing various household jobs. This was not something I would have even considered before, but it seemed perfect. I needed work, I didn't want to be traditionally employed, and they needed the help. It was perfect for both of us.

Before long, word had spread and I was cleaning half a dozen houses a week, doing odd bits of gardening, building furniture, and any heavy lifting that people needed hired help for. It was quite a bizarre few months as I started to make more than enough to live on from a selection of jobs that were generally flexible enough so that I could chop and change where I was on any given day.

This was immensely liberating, and even though I wasn't doing what I wanted to do forever, there was a real sense of integrity in the fact that I was doing work from a point of need and was supported by my various "clients" so that I had the time and flexibility to build on my music without worrying about making money from it.

It's been four years since Andy began his Slash career and in that time he has narrowed down his portfolio to four slashes (one of which is his musical career—he's currently recording his fifth album). Andy is no longer involved in a dozen odd jobs, but the experiences and the self-knowledge he acquired during that time led him to where he is today. Although he fell into it unintentionally, the Slash Approach was a natural fit for Andy. He dislikes working in hierarchical structures, values freedom and flexibility, and is open to new experiences. Andy's story also illustrates the power of the Slash Approach to support a blossoming artistic career.

RUNNING MULTIPLE BUSINESSES

In the previous chapter, we talked about how multipotential-ites sometimes find variety by owning a single, broad business (called a Renaissance Business). Another way to satisfy the need for variety is to run a few narrow businesses that each provide a specialized service. Shanna Mann owns three discrete businesses:

1. Bookselling—Hunting down books at local book sales and selling them online.

2. Coaching—Helping small business owners with systematization and administration.

3. Content Generation—Creating articles about search engine optimization for technology websites.

Like the other multipotentialites we've met, each of Shanna's slashes results in a different amount of meaning and money. Her book-selling business brings in the bulk of her income and appeals to her love of treasure hunting. Her content generation business is highly systematized at this point, and she outsources a lot of the writing so it's an easy source of revenue. Her coaching business is the least stable of her income streams—she may have many clients in a given month and very few the next—but she adores working individually with entrepreneurs and helping them find order and sustainability in their businesses. The work is meaningful, and the irregular revenue isn't a problem because her other two businesses are so reliable.

Trying on the Slash Approach

Now that we've gotten a feel for the Slash Approach, let's see how your work life might look if you were to pursue several of your passions at one time. Grab a pen and paper. It's time to generate and match up some slashes!

CREATE YOUR MASTER LIST OF INTERESTS

(If you did this when you went through Chapter 4, you don't need to do it again. Just pull out your master list and skip to the Further Refine Your List section on page 100.)

Write down every interest, passion, skill, and curiosity, past and present, that you can think of. Do not censor yourself. It doesn't matter if you aren't currently involved in the activity, or if it's a very new or fleeting interest. When completing exercises like these, we have a tendency to discredit our accomplishments, so try to adhere to this rule: if at any point during this exercise, you wonder whether or not to include something, include it.

REFINE YOUR LIST

Cross out your "dead" interests—the items on your list that you have no desire to touch again anytime soon. Star the items on your list that sound especially exciting to you right now.

FURTHER REFINE YOUR LIST

Take a look at your master list and underline the items:

- that you've been paid for in the past,

- for which you possess a higher-than-average level of expertise, and

- that you know to be lucrative.

MAKE A LIST OF POSSIBLE SLASHES / REVENUE STREAMS

On a new sheet of paper, write down each of your starred and underlined interests, leaving plenty of space beneath each one. Under each interest, make a list of slashes / revenue streams that sound appealing. This could include: part-time jobs, services you could offer, products you could create, random project ideas, and so on. Your page might look something like the example on the opposite page.

Don't be afraid to include slashes that feel difficult or impractical. It's important to get all your ideas out of your head and onto the page, so tell your inner critic to take a hike if it's giving you a hard time.

ARE THESE SLASHES IN LINE WITH YOUR WHYS?

Compare each of the slashes on your page to your Whys that you identified in Chapter 3. Is each slash in line with one or more of your Whys? Or does considering this slash bring up new Whys?

FASHION

- Custom tailoring
- Costume designer
- Freelance fashion journalist
- Start online clothing company

EDUCATION

- Substitute teacher
- Run workshops for an organization
- Curriculum designer
- Math tutor
- Museum docent

FICTION WRITING

- Get fantasy novel published (or self-publish)
- Writing coach
- Lead writing workshops
- Start small press
- Create monthly storytelling event

PSYCHOLOGY

- Counselor
- Write memoir about experiences related to mental health
- Build app that helps people improve their self-esteem

HORTICULTURE

- Landscaping business
- Arborist
- Start community garden

TRY PUTTING YOUR SLASHES TOGETHER

On a new piece of paper, write down two to five slashes that sound exciting to you and consider how they fit together. Some questions to ask:

- Are these slashes different from one another, such that each slash will add something unique to my life?

- Will these slashes provide me with enough (but not too much) variety?

- When combined, will these slashes provide me with enough income to meet my financial goals?

- Is this combination of slashes compatible with my Perfect Day?[7]

You might not be able to answer these questions with much accuracy now. Moving from a dream Slash career to a real-life, thriving Slash career involves a lot of experimentation. You won't know whether a particular set of slashes will provide you with the money, meaning, and variety you need until you try it out. Still, it's worth using the knowledge you have about yourself and about your goals to point you in the right direction. You can course-correct later.

KEEP PLAYING WITH DIFFERENT COMBINATIONS

Put together different combinations of the slashes you identified, and run those combinations through the questions in the previous section.

TAKING ACTION

If you're excited about pursuing a Slash career, decide on one to three small action steps that you can take this week to get started. Your action steps will depend on your situation and the nature of your slashes, but here are a few possible examples:

- Contact specific people in your network (friends, family, teachers, colleagues, etc.) who might have leads or connections to help you break in to one of your slashes.

7. As discussed in Chapter 3.

- Research the market viability of one of your business ideas. Is there a need for this product/service? Who is your audience?

- E-mail someone who has one of the slashes you're considering and see if they'd be willing to answer a few of your questions.

KEY POINTS FROM THIS CHAPTER

The Slash work model allows us to express our different facets frequently and fluidly. It's a good option for multipotentialites who love juggling multiple projects at once. Here are the key takeaways from this chapter:

- The Slash Approach is having two or more part-time jobs and/or businesses that you flit between on a regular basis.

- Part-time is the dream. You love each of your slashes but wouldn't want to do any one of them full-time.

- Each slash adds something special to your life and challenges you in a different way.

- Slashing allows you to work in specialized fields and tap into niche markets without burning out or getting bored.

- The Slash work model provides a flexible schedule when compared to full-time employment. This makes it a good fit for many artists.

- Slash careerists are typically self-directed and have an independent or entrepreneurial spirit.

- Multipotentialites often begin their journey into Slash careerdom by: (1) transitioning from a full-time job to a part-time version of the same job, (2) accepting a part-time opportunity that becomes slash #1, and/or (3) diving into numerous slashes and refining them later.

THE EINSTEIN APPROACH

For almost a decade in the early 1900s, Albert Einstein worked as a patent officer for the Swiss government. Despite his day job, he managed to produce some of his most notable work during this period, including his special theory of relativity. How did Einstein find the time to have a full-time job *and* develop his theories? Yes, we all know that Einstein was a genius, but his ability to pursue his "personal projects" (read: world-changing scientific endeavors) had little to do with his exquisite mind and *everything* to do with his chosen work model. Einstein's position at the patent office granted him security and financial stability. Being a patent officer was also a notoriously slow-paced job that left him with ample time and energy at the end of the day to work on his theories. As an added benefit, he got to learn about new inventions at work every day. Einstein had a "good enough job," a term I'm borrowing from Barbara Sher and her book *Refuse to Choose!*[1]

The Einstein Approach is having one full-time job or business that fully supports you, while leaving you with enough time and energy to pursue your other passions on the side. In other words, the Einstein work model lets you *be* everything without having to *monetize* everything. It's a good choice for people who want to (comfortably) pursue a field that doesn't normally come with a big paycheck.

STIFLING OR LIBERATING?

The Einstein Approach is not for everybody. For some of us, the idea of relegating our multipotentiality to evenings and week- ends is unacceptable. We would rather starve than spend forty hours a week doing something we can't pour our whole selves into. Yet for many, the Einstein Approach is nothing short of liberating. By removing the pressure of having to generate in- come from every interest, we free ourselves to explore without worry. We can jump from field to field, project to project, and whim to whim. We can add or drop things as we please—no questions asked, no financial repercussions.

1. There is some debate over whether Albert Einstein was a true polymath or just a genius. (I am laughing about having written the words *just a genius*.) Einstein once said, "I have no special talent. I am only passionately curious." In addition to science, he loved music and played the violin. Regardless of Einstein's genius-and-or-multipotentialite status, the way he lived his life can teach us something about structuring our work so that it supports our multiple passions.

Whether the Einstein Approach appeals to you will depend in part on how much you value stability versus flexibility. Most of the Slash careerists we met in Chapter 5 craved a high degree of flexibility and independence. Many had left traditional jobs because that world wasn't a good fit for them. Happy Einsteiners, on the other hand, value stability. They tend to like the structure, routine, and camaraderie that can be found in a workplace. Though being palatable to society at large isn't usually their primary motivation, the Einstein model provides an added benefit of having an easy-to-understand job title and generally making sense to the world. Multipotentialites who take the Einstein Approach are unlikely to confuse others when introducing themselves at a party. What differentiates them from most people isn't how they pay the bills. It's the colorful array of other hobbies and passions in their lives.

As an IT manager, Charlie Harper is in the office five days a week, from 8:30 to 5:30. When he leaves in the evening, he sometimes swings by his house to have dinner with his three children—he alternates responsibility for dinner duty so that he's free several evenings per week—and sometimes heads directly to musical theater or a cappella practice. In addition to being an arts enthusiast, Charlie is a professional-grade amateur carpenter. He once built a house with his father and has constructed numerous pieces of furniture. When we spoke, he had just completed a boat.

Charlie's job as an IT manager puts him in close contact with technology, one of his longtime loves. Although he isn't able to integrate his every interest and skill into his work, Charlie's job allows him to perform a range of tasks within the technology sector. In his words, "If it plugs in, it's my domain. My work touches every facet of the business because computers are so integral to our operations." Charlie also taps into his multipotentialite superpowers by taking advantage of learning opportunities at work. "Right now my big kick is security. I've got a stack of hacking books on my desk and I'm reading through a bunch of certification articles."

Though Charlie loves performing arts and carpentry, he chose not to pursue either field professionally. His local community theater, his singing group, and the odd building project enrich his life and bring him great fulfillment. He has no desire to monetize these activities. Doing so might actually make them less fun. The IT job helps pay the bills, while the hobbies fulfill Charlie's creative side. There's no pressure for the side interests to earn him money, and no pressure for the IT work to be his passion in life. Charlie has been at his company for fourteen years, and even though it might not be his be-all and end-all *multipotentialite dream job,* it allows him to support his family and he enjoys it. And when the workday ends, it ends. He isn't expected to stay late at the office. He can take off and have fun with his other multipotentialite projects. His job might not be thrilling, but it's good enough.

WHAT MAKES A JOB GOOD ENOUGH?

As an aspiring Einsteiner, you should make sure that the job you're considering is good enough, because if it isn't—if it is just barely tolerable or doesn't allow you to meet your basic needs—then you will not be happy.

To qualify as good enough, a job must fulfill three criteria:

1. Be enjoyable, preferably even challenging and fun, and in an area in which you have genuine interest. A good enough job does not need to be multifaceted, though it can be (this is where the good enough job and the Group Hug job begin to blend—more on this in a moment).

2. Have a high enough salary to allow you to meet your financial goals.[2]

3. Leave you with enough free time and energy to pursue your other interests outside of work. If it takes up eighty hours of your week or you feel completely drained at the end of the day, it is *not* good enough.

Speaking as a Canadian-American millennial, this conversation has to include an acknowledgment of how much has changed since Barbara Sher started talking about the good enough job. Job security is disappearing. Employees are working more hours for less pay. Many of us are expected to answer work e-mails late into the night. And let's not forget about the crippling student debt that many young people face. Despite these challenges, I believe that the good enough job still exists. It's just harder to come by.

FINDING THE ENERGY

How do Einsteiners have the stamina to go from a full day at the office to, say, musical theater practice? It isn't a coincidence that

2. As defined by you in Chapter 3.

Charlie's hobbies are very different from his paid work. While IT allows Charlie to tap into his analytical and problem-solving skills, his hobbies are more intuitive, artistic, and body centered. He is reenergized by the shift from a logical to an intuitive mode that takes place when he transitions from job to hobby. If his day job were something more physically taxing, he might spend his nights learning programming rather than harmonizing in five parts. As it stands, Charlie has no interest in developing his programming skills after work. It would be too similar to what he does all day long. So, musical theater it is! When considering a potential good enough job, think about how similar it is to your other interests. Does it tap into the same skills and modes of thought? If so, will too much of the same thing make it hard to sustain your focus as you shift from a full workday into your personal projects?

VARIETY: WHEN LESS IS MORE . . .

Many Einsteiners have jobs that allow them to wear a few different hats. Is the good enough job simply an inferior version of a Group Hug job? Isn't *more variety* always better? Not necessarily. There are several reasons that you might prefer to have a less multifaceted day job.

April Vomfell left her job as a librarian because she felt it was too taxing—although she enjoyed the work, it seemed like it was using up all her time and energy. She has transitioned into working as a web editor, which she describes as "narrower and more boring." For April (and for the time being), this is perfect.

The upside to a rote and limited job is the ability to leave her work at work:

> Without stress following me home, I'm spending my free time working on a side project with my husband. We have a small farm and I've been growing and selling flowers, and loving it. Thanks to my day job, and the fact that these changes were my choice, I am much happier these days.

I'd venture to say that April's previous job as a librarian wasn't good enough, at least not for her.[3] It didn't provide her with the time and energy to pursue her passion projects on the side, because the job was too all-consuming. April poured so much of herself into her work—tapped into so many different skills and interests—that she was maxed out at the end of the day. Choosing between the Group Hug Approach and the Einstein Approach is really a choice between getting your variety built in at work or getting it on your own time and terms.

THE GOOD ENOUGH BUSINESS

The self-employment version of the Einstein Approach involves running one narrow, lucrative business that provides sufficient income and leaves you with enough time to pursue your other

---

3. I've spoken with many multipotentialites who adore their jobs in library science for exactly the reason that April didn't: they get to do and be many things.

passions. It's an approach that works well for multipotentialites who possess a specialized skill that is in high demand. Technological skills like programming, web development, or graphic design tend to make strong good enough businesses. Consulting is another narrow offering that can be quite lucrative.

Leigh Matthews works as a freelance science writer. She spends thirty hours a week transforming complicated medical journal articles into short, pithy summaries. Like Charlie's, Leigh's paid work is multifaceted without being all-consuming (either conceptually or temporally). She writes about several medical topics and often brings her nonmedical interests into her work. For example, a few years ago, she worked with a surgeon who performs gender reassignment surgery. At the time, he was finding it difficult to locate a medical writer who could write about these procedures in a knowledgeable and sympathetic way. Leigh is an ace science writer with backgrounds in LGBTQ activism and social justice; she was the perfect person to help him create brochures for people undergoing transition surgery. Leigh finds other ways to inject these interests into her work on a regular basis. She loves altering gendered language to make articles more inclusive—she might change "women who are pregnant" to "those who are pregnant"—and she often finds herself clarifying the difference between gender and sex in her writing.

Leigh enjoys the challenge of turning a five-thousand-word article into a few hundred words. She loves the "solving a puzzle" quality of playing with language. Yet, despite the fun and somewhat interdisciplinary nature of her business, she has interests that she does not tap into at work. Her paid work is about communicating in a very particular style. Her unpaid work is more artistic and collaborative: she's currently writing a novel, collaborating with a composer to turn one of her books into an opera, and creating a chapbook of poetry analogizing beers and relationships.[4]

THE RELATIVE VALUE OF SKILLS

Financial stability is key in the Einstein Approach. It's what empowers you to explore your passions on the side without worry. Using the Einstein Approach means having a job or owning a business that brings in enough money to support you. For better or worse, there will always be skills that are both rarer and in greater demand than others. These skills command a higher paycheck. It's not surprising, then, that the three Einsteiners we've met so far have technical and information-based jobs. It also isn't a coincidence that neither Leigh nor Charlie are paid much (if anything) for their more artistic work. Artistic pursuits, although socially important and personally gratifying, can be difficult to monetize. You are unlikely to find someone whose good enough job is, say, theater directing. Theater directors usually do it for passion, not for security, and put a lot of their soul and time into the work.

If you have artistic aspirations, don't worry. You don't have to give them up or be a starving artist. You can get your security elsewhere (in a field in which you're also genuinely interested) and pursue your art in your free time, or skip the Einstein Approach and go with something else, like the Slash

---

4. She got the idea for the project when she was out with a friend. She took a sip of her drink and thought, *This beer is like a relationship. It's got an exciting start and then it's full bodied and then it has a sort of angsty, bitter finish.*

Approach. These strategies don't make you a sellout. One of the beautiful things about being a multipotentialite is that we possess a range of skills and interests. The Einstein Approach allows us to identify and build good enough jobs around our more profitable skills so that we can pursue our other interests pressure-free.

GOOD ENOUGH JOBS AND PROFESSIONAL TRAINING

What if you're interested in having a good enough job that requires years of training? Matt Lambert is a seventy-two-year-old physician who has been working in the medical field for forty-seven years! He was a surgeon in private practice and a professor of surgery for most of his career and he more recently moved into the area of hospital executive management. If you were to read about Matt's forty-seven-year medical career in any other context, you might not think he was a multipotentialite at all. Medicine is considered by many to be the holy grail of specialist careers.[5]

But even doctors can be multipotentialites, and multipotentialites with an interest in medicine need not be discouraged about heading down that path. Matt may be a physician by trade, but he is also a passionate artist, avid reader, and lifelong learner. When describing his life as a surgeon, he said,

---

5. Spoiler alert: this is a misconception.

I liked being a doctor but I continued to write (short stories, poems, and one novel); I played in a band and played guitar; did wood carving, block printing, Chinese brush paintings, collages, acrylic painting, medieval illuminations, wire sculpture; and continued to read voraciously.

Matt is one of the most inspiring people I interviewed for this book. At seventy-two, he is unapologetic about prioritizing his personal projects, and he schedules his free time with great intentionality:

Life is too short for frustration or unfulfilled expectations and, even though we can't accomplish everything we would like, we can do a lot better. I try to carve out time every day for things that are important to me: meditating, reading, creating, thinking, and appreciating all the world has to offer, including family and friends.

Matt wasn't always so confident about having multiple passions. He used to view his interests in medicine and the arts as incompatible:

I kept thinking I had missed the boat being a doctor and was still searching for what I really was to be. I never thought that maybe this (being a multipotentialite) is what I was meant to do until recently.

Trying on the Einstein Approach

Would following Einstein's example and establishing a good enough job or business be a good fit for you? Let's consider your particular skills, interests, and goals and see what your life might look like if you were to use the Einstein Approach.

CREATE YOUR MASTER LIST OF INTERESTS

(If you did this when you went through Chapter 4, you don't need to do it again. Just pull out your master list and skip to the Make a List of Possible Good Enough Jobs section below.)

Write down every interest, passion, skill, and curiosity, past and present, that you can think of. Do not censor yourself. It doesn't matter if you aren't currently involved in the activity, or if it's a very new or fleeting interest. When completing exercises like these, we have a tendency to discredit our accomplishments, so try to adhere to this rule: if at any point during this exercise, you wonder whether or not to include something, include it.

REFINE YOUR LIST

Cross out your "dead" interests—the items on your list that you have no desire to touch again anytime soon. Star the items on your list that sound especially exciting to you right now.

MAKE A LIST OF POSSIBLE GOOD ENOUGH JOBS

Imagine you were to speak with a career adviser (or actually go speak with one). What careers might they suggest after looking at your master list of interests? Do some research to see what jobs are recommended for someone with your particular background(s). Careers that are commonly perceived of as being "practical" often make decent good enough jobs. For example, if you do a quick search for "jobs for sociology majors," you'll find numerous career suggestions, including social researcher, actuarial analyst, and UX (user experience) analyst. And if you look up "careers related to sports," you'll find things like fitness director, exercise physiologist, and sports dietitian.

DOUBLE-CHECK TO MAKE SURE THAT EACH JOB YOU DISCOVERED IS, IN FACT, GOOD ENOUGH

For each potential good enough job you identified, ask the following questions:

- Would this job provide me with enough income to meet the financial goals I defined in Chapter 3?

- How many hours of my week would this job occupy?

- Would this job be creatively, emotionally, or physically draining?

- Would this job provide me with opportunities to learn at work?

- Does this job sound like fun? Do I foresee myself liking my employer, my colleagues, and the environment in which I would be working?

- Is this job different enough from the other projects I would like to pursue? Does it use different skills and modes of thought?

- What would my day and week look like if I were to have this job and engage with my other passions on the side? Is this schedule compatible with my Perfect Day that I conceived of in Chapter 3?

Each job doesn't need to score perfectly on all these criteria and you probably won't be able to answer all these questions in the abstract, anyway. However, these questions are important to think about as you consider potential good enough jobs.

MAKE A LIST OF POSSIBLE GOOD ENOUGH BUSINESSES

Take a look at your master list. What skills do you have that people might pay you for? Don't worry if you aren't yet at a level where you feel you could pursue all these skills professionally. We're just brainstorming here, so get all your ideas out on paper now. You will be growing, changing, and refining forever, so there is no need to limit yourself.

HOW LUCRATIVE ARE THE SKILLS YOU IDENTIFIED ABOVE?

For each of the skills you identified, ask:

- How well does/can this skill pay?

- To what extent is this skill in demand?

- How rare is this skill?

- Is there a particular niche you could fill or an audience that would pay more for this skill? (E.g., freelance marketing for larger companies might pay better than working with small businesses or nonprofits.)

PUTTING IT TOGETHER

On a new sheet of paper, make a list of the good enough job and business ideas you've generated throughout these exercises.

TAKING ACTION

If you're excited about pursuing an Einstein career, decide on one to three small action steps that you can take this week to move you in the right direction. Your action steps will depend on your situation and the nature of your good enough job and business ideas, but here are a few possible examples:

- Contact someone who works in a profession you're considering and ask them about the day-to-day realities of the job.

- Practice/improve one of your potentially lucrative skills.

- Revise your résumé so that it reflects your experience and qualifications for a good enough job that you're serious about going for.

KEY POINTS FROM THIS CHAPTER

The Einstein Approach is a great option for multipotentialites who are content (or relieved) to be engaging with their interests purely for fun and on their own terms. It's also a good fit for those who thrive with stability and routine. Here are the main points we discussed in this chapter:

- The Einstein Approach is having one full-time job or business that fully supports you, while leaving you with enough time and energy to pursue your other passions on the side.

- The Einstein Approach involves having a good enough job. If you'd prefer to be self-employed, you could start your own good enough business.

- For a job or business to be good enough, it must provide: (1) enjoyment, (2) sufficient income, and (3) free time.

- Einsteiners find the energy to go from their paid work to their passion work by ensuring that the two use different skill sets and modes of thought.

- Some people seek out good enough jobs that are multifaceted in nature. However, too much variety can sometimes be counterproductive as it can make it harder to sustain your energy after work. If an interdisciplinary job sounds more appealing, be sure to check out the Group Hug work model.

- Since financial stability is a key component of the Einstein Approach, our more lucrative skills translate best into good enough jobs/businesses.

- It's okay to be interested in a profession that requires years of training. There are plenty of multipotentialites who complement their passion for a field that requires years of study with numerous meaningful and unrelated hobbies.

THE PHOENIX APPROACH

The phoenix is among the most famous of mythical creatures. According to legend, the large red-and-gold bird lives for upward of five hundred years. At the end of this life, it builds a pyre of twigs and—here's where the various mythical interpretations diverge—either bursts into flames or lies down, dies, and decomposes slowly. The phoenix is then reborn from its ashes (or its primordial muck . . .).

The phoenix is an apt metaphor for some of us. While some multipotentialites thrive when they have multiple active interests in their lives, others become fascinated by a single subject for months or even years.[1] *The Phoenix Approach is working in a*

1. If this sounds like you, you are not disqualified from calling yourself a multipotentialite.

single industry for several months or years and then shifting gears and starting a new career in a new industry. Unsurprisingly, this career model works best for multipotentialites who fall closer to the sequential end of the simultaneous–sequential spectrum[2] and enjoy exploring their passions one at a time.

I met Trever Clark through a mutual friend shortly after launching my website, Puttylike. At the time, Trever was a passionate blogger and digital marketer. Even though he was living in Michigan and I was living in Denmark at the time, we became fast friends online, exchanging advice and support as we grew our respective blogs. He was actually the first person to use the word *multipotentialite!*[3] As often happens with friends who live far apart, Trever and I lost touch over the next few years but kept general tabs on each other over social media. At one point, I noticed that the subject of his updates had changed. Instead of sharing technology articles, Trever was now enthusiastically posting about food—namely the artisan mushroom farm he had started with a friend. They were growing gourmet mushrooms and selling them to local upscale restaurants.

Shortly after I learned of Trever's new career, my wife and I were on a road trip. We decided to make a stop to catch up and see his headquarters at The Urban Mushroom. The space was impressive. There were entire rooms of enormous, colorful mushrooms, many of varieties I'd never heard of. But I was most struck by how passionate Trever was about mycology. (He recounted his recent adventures while carefully spraying a

2. As discussed in Chapter 1.

3. I had discussed the psychological term *multipotentiality* on my blog, and Trever graciously published a blog post on his site suggesting his readers check out my work. In this post, he referred to the community at Puttylike as being comprised of "multipotentialites." It stuck. (He gave me permission to run with it.)

wall of lion's manes.) The same enthusiasm he had once poured into online marketing was totally present, only this time it was applied to petri dish experiments, not keyword research.

Fast-forward three years: I wasn't surprised to learn that Trever had sold his share of the mushroom business and had become the director of operations for a local food exchange. A year after that, he moved on to become a technical support analyst. Trever is a multipotentialite who moves through his interests sequentially (one at a time). He becomes fascinated with something and dives in with total abandon—for a few years. Once he no longer feels challenged, he leaves it behind and moves on to a new field. Each time he reaches his personal end point, his old identity erupts into a glorious blaze and he is reborn from the ashes to step into a new role.

FINDING A BALANCE BETWEEN DEPTH AND BREADTH

The Phoenix work model is best suited for multipotentialites who like to go deep and who don't require a lot of variety in their lives to be happy. The Phoenix Approach differs from every other work model in one significant way: it doesn't provide you with variety—or rather the variety it provides happens very slowly: you only see it when looking back at your work history. When you venture into an area of interest, you probably aren't engaging with many of your other interests at the same time. You explore things one after the next, after the next, often with several years (as opposed to hours) between each switch. If you fall close to the sequential end of the simultaneous-sequential spectrum, the Phoenix Approach could be right for you.

The Abandoned Ph.D. Theory

Here's a fun fact from my research: compared to multipotentialites who use other work models, Phoenix multipotentialites disproportionately have at least one abandoned Ph.D. program in their pasts. Possible socioeconomic factors aside, many Phoenixes report loving their advanced, five-year academic programs for roughly three or four of those years and then losing interest.

Bart Lenselink decided to leave his Ph.D. program in chemistry after four years. He had become bored and lost the drive to continue his thesis. After leaving, Bart decided to pursue his love of computers, which turned into a thirty-year career during which he moved through marketing, telecommunications, IT process architecture, project management, and management consulting. Similarly, Stéphanie Lebrun Kohler chose not to finish her Ph.D. in journalism. A few years in, she was more than ready to try something new. Stéphanie ended up getting a job in advertising and then transitioned to education and then translation. This pattern of Phoenix multipotentialites pursuing and then abandoning advanced degrees makes perfect sense. They are so fascinated by a certain field that they go after the highest attainable level of education, but they don't want to maintain that level of dedication for such an extended period of time. Does that make them failures? Heck no. They're Phoenixes. More than any other type of multipotentialite, Phoenixes love to go deep. But like all multipotentialites, they also need to feel excited and challenged by their work.

What If You Need More Variety?

Let's say you aren't quite as laser focused as the Phoenixes we've met so far. One way to make the Phoenix Approach more multifaceted is to combine work models and/or build in a progressive way between successive models to get you gradually where you want to be. Consider, for example, a multipotentialite who moves from engineering to health to food over a period of ten years. As an engineer, this person uses the Einstein Approach and has a good enough job at a large company while exploring their other passions on the side. Once they transition to health, they take a Slash Approach and establish multiple part-time revenue streams, each of which is related to health in some way: they assist at a clinic a few days per week, provide nutrition coaching for a handful of clients, and teach yoga. Finally, upon moving into the food industry, they use the Group Hug Approach and start a gluten-free bakery, which becomes their Renaissance Business, as it combines their interests in health and food. They even set up their bakery in a space that is large enough to accommodate the occasional yoga class.

By combining the Phoenix Approach with other work models, you can go deeper into one thing for longer periods of time without closing off your world to other interests. But when it is time to change paths, that change isn't usually as abrupt or arbitrary as it can look from the outside.

A PHOENIX'S REBIRTH IS RARELY RANDOM

To casual acquaintances, it might look like Phoenix multipotentialites are all over the map—randomly morphing between professional identities. Take the story I shared at the beginning of the book about bumping into my ex-acting teacher. She was confused by my seemingly random metamorphosis from filmmaker to lawyer. Although our various incarnations can appear random and disjointed, there is often a common Why (or Whys, plural) underlying them. In this case, my Why had to do with a love of problem solving. As it turns out, problem solving is a big part of both producing a film and unpacking complicated legal cases.

Sometimes, a challenging personal experience can inspire a Why and that Why can, in turn, shape the particular fields and careers we are drawn to. Mariah Wilberg has reinvented herself more than a few times. She began her career as a workshop facilitator for domestic violence prevention. She then moved on to work in the area of preventing sex trafficking and sexual exploitation. Within a year, she was offered a job at an HIV/AIDS organization and she has now been working as a health educator and speaker for four years. When we spoke, Mariah had the urge to shake things up again. She was no longer feeling challenged at her job and was thinking about starting a career in criminal justice. Mariah's biggest reinvention, however, isn't any of these career moves. It happened before any of this and is a lot more personal. Mariah struggled with alcohol and drug addiction in her late teens. She was in an abusive relationship, and she eventually ended up homeless and then incarcerated. During her time in prison, Mariah began working on herself—she started therapy, journaled every day, and read over one hundred personal development books—and giving back through volunteering. She decided that she was going to turn her life around and dedicate her career to "helping the people who slip through the cracks," the way she had. This is Mariah's Why, and it informs *everything* she does professionally, from domestic violence reduction, to HIV/AIDS education, to criminal justice. It doesn't matter what form her work takes, it's all about helping those who are in trouble and lacking support and resources.

Can you spot some common threads that run through the various roles, projects, and identities you've had over the years? Each transition helps you explore your Why(s) in a different way. Which brings us to the next question: What if you're ready to burst into flames and rise from the ashes again?

HOW TO KNOW WHEN TO SWITCH FIELDS

As a Phoenix multipotentialite, one of the biggest challenges is knowing when to say good-bye to a particular path and move on to something new. Author and business coach Pamela Slim developed a clever technique that you can use to determine the right time to change positions, companies, or industries. She calls it "the loathing scale." Imagine a ruler that goes from 1 to 10. At 1, everything's great and you love your job. At 10, you feel physically ill even thinking about walking into your workplace. Think for a moment about where you're at on the scale in your own job right now. Pam has found that, for most people, the best time to switch is in the 5–8 range (she calls this "the angst range"). If you wait until you are in the 9–10 range (the point at which you feel exhausted, sick, and depressed), you probably won't make a very graceful exit. You might be so desperate to escape at that point that you burn bridges, quit rashly, or make dubious career choices by jumping into something else simply because it sounds better. The best way to know where you fall on the loathing scale is to check in with yourself regularly and to pay attention to how you feel in your body.[4] Seasoned Phoenix multipotentialites know the "angst range" well, and this is when they begin looking into new options.

Even more than intense anger or stress, the word that multipotentialites often use to describe the dawning awareness that it's time to move on is *boredom*. You lose your patience easily and find that you no longer feel excited or challenged. Perhaps you have lost the desire to initiate projects, whereas in the past you always had ideas you wanted to pitch to your boss. These are some of the signs that it's time to think about

---

4. How does this feel? Here's how Pam describes it: "Physically, you notice your energy goes up and down. You have some high-energy good days when you get stuff done, but overall you feel slightly annoyed to highly stressed when you head to the office."

the next phase of your career and begin setting the stage for a transition.

EXPLORE ON THE SIDE BEFORE YOU JUMP

It's beautiful and dramatic to think about a majestic phoenix bursting into flames. Yet, when it comes to our careers, a healthier model to follow is the version of the myth in which the phoenix dies naturally and decomposes slowly before emerging again. So instead of thinking about your transition as one door closing (or slamming shut and bursting into flames), think about how you can make the most of this limbo period. Most Phoenix multipotentialites grow their knowledge, experience, and contacts on the side before jumping from one career to the next. Laying a foundation before quitting your job leads to a smoother transition. In fact, exploring on the side is often what makes the transition possible at all, since it exposes you to professional opportunities.

REINVENTING YOURSELF: TIPS FOR A SMOOTH TRANSITION

Imagine you're working in a field that you once found inspiring. You loved your job for the first few years—it fit with your interests, provided plenty of learning opportunities, and was in line with your Whys. Over the last six or twelve months, however, you've become increasingly impatient at work. Tasks that once felt like fun challenges are now rote and uninspiring. But there's this other thing . . . this different area that has piqued your curiosity and that you've been learning about for a while now. You start to think: *Maybe I can find a job related to my new passion! That sounds incredible.* Where do you start? How do you break into an industry you've never worked in before? And how do you compete with other candidates who have education and professional experience in this space? Here are six strategies to help you break into a new field.

1. Reach Out to Your Existing Network

When it comes to landing a job, relationships matter more than résumés. I'm not talking about nepotism here, and I'm not suggesting that your résumé doesn't count. It's just that there's nothing quite as powerful as a personal recommendation from someone your future employer trusts. Do you know anyone who works in the industry or in an adjacent one? Do you have any friends who are natural connectors, meaning they know a lot of random and interesting people? Reach out to people in your life to see who can help with an introduction or a recommendation.

2. Expand Your Network

Go to events related to your new interest, attend lectures, and try to meet new people. Before I go on, let me address the elephant in the room—and that's you, introverts. I get it. I'm an introvert, too. I get overwhelmed in crowds; the word *networking* makes me shudder. But you know what I love? I love learning about other human beings. I love hearing stories and understanding what makes someone tick. It's just that I prefer to do this in a quiet, one-on-one setting, rather than at a bustling networking function. If you're an introvert, here's what I suggest: Go to the events, but don't stay long. While you're there, will yourself to mingle. You can always be up front about how awkward you find these kinds of things. There's a good chance that someone within earshot will let out a sigh of relief and say, *me too!* (I've made more than a few friends this way.) Escape when you become overwhelmed and then get in touch with anyone you met who could be a potential friend or colleague. Offer to take them out for coffee, or if they live far away, suggest a Skype date. Actively seeking out new contacts can have a profound effect on your professional opportunities.

3. Volunteer

Volunteering can give you practical experience, develop your skills, and allow you to give back. You'll get to meet people who are working in the industry. They know about job openings, can act as references, or may even hire you themselves one day. Mariah is an avid volunteer. She currently serves on a board of directors and is an active volunteer for four or five different causes or agencies. Volunteering puts her in the right place at the right time and connects her to the right people. It has resulted in more than a few job offers.

4. Do "Free Work"

This approach is especially effective if you want to establish a freelance career. In his book *Recession-Proof Graduate,* Charlie

Hoehn champions the idea of doing "free work." Here's how it works: you seek out a small business owner that you'd like to work with and you offer to help for free. Eventually, after doing a fantastic job and delighting your "client" with your unpaid talent, you propose transitioning to a paid arrangement (with no hard feelings if it doesn't work out).

Charlie recommends figuring out who you'd like to work with, sending them an e-mail outlining something you believe they could use help with, and then offering to do that work for them for free. Pitching yourself requires research, specificity, and some up-front effort. In an article for *Forbes,* Charlie explains how he approached *New York Times* bestselling author Ramit Sethi:

> For Ramit, I said, "You're really good on video, but you don't do enough video. I bet that's because it's really arduous and time-consuming, so if you shoot video, I'll edit them and upload them, and you don't have to think about it. And here's a video I've already compiled of you speaking, which you can use as a demo to land more speaking gigs."

This was an offer Sethi couldn't refuse and they soon began working together.

How do you make your offer irresistible to the person you're hoping to work with? I can say that I've been on the receiving end of e-mails like this over the years. I usually say no, and the reason is always some combination of the following:

- *The offer isn't specific or isn't something I need/want help with right now.* How exactly are you going to help? Are you offering to do something that I care about and that we aren't already doing?

- *It's going to require too much work on my part to set up or train the person in our system.* Have you done this before? How do I know I can trust you? If you're offering to help with graphic design, do you have a portfolio online? If you want to help with writing, do you have a blog I can check out? Have you used WordPress before?

- *I don't know who the person is.* This might be industry-specific, but at Puttylike there are plenty of opportunities to get involved. I recognize the names of people who regularly comment on blog posts or offer advice in the forums. If I recognize your name, I'm more likely to seriously consider your pitch. When I hire people for my team, they are almost always active and helpful members of the community. I've noticed their particular aptitudes (and awesome personalities) and I want them on my team.

In sum: do your homework, know your audience, offer something valuable, make sure your offer doesn't require any upfront work on the part of the person you're pitching, and (if possible) get involved first.

5. Get Some Training

Taking a class or getting a certification can develop your skills, connect you with people who share your passion, and bolster your résumé. Some careers have licensure requirements and/or require advanced degrees. If this is the case, and it makes sense from a financial perspective, then enrolling in an academic program is certainly an option. However, if the career you're pursuing doesn't require an advanced degree, then consider taking classes in your area or online.

6. Emphasize Your Transferable Skills

It's easy to feel like you're at a disadvantage when you apply for a job in a new industry. One way to compete with candidates who have more training and experience is to stress your transferable skills. Explain how your past work experiences relate to the job at hand. In her cover letter for a paralegal position (for which she had zero experience), Mariah Wilberg described the relevant skills she uses in her nonprofit career: she works under pressure, meets strict deadlines, adheres to grant requirements, works with emotional clients, and so on.[5]

When starting over in a new field, know that you may have to take a few steps back on the professional ladder. Be humble and be open to learning. Show your enthusiasm. You might move up faster than you think. If relationships trump résumés, then surely enthusiasm can surpass experience.[6]

GRACEFUL GOOD-BYES

When leaving your job to pursue a new adventure, there will probably be people who are impacted by your departure. Try

5. She was offered the job but she ultimately decided to go in a different direction.
6. As long as you're not a surgeon.

to honor the commitments you've made, and do what you can to make the transition as smooth as possible for those who rely on you, including your employer, coworkers, and clients. That might mean giving your boss a decent amount of notice, sticking around for an extra few weeks to complete a project you've been working on, or helping to train your replacement, if appropriate.

SERIAL ENTREPRENEURSHIP

Of course, some sassy Phoenixes want to be their own boss. What do you call a self-employed Phoenix? (Pretend you didn't see the heading for this section.) That's right: a serial entrepreneur! A serial entrepreneur starts a business, grows it to a point of profitability, and then steps away to some degree—either by selling it or hiring people to help run it. Then, they start a new company in a new industry and begin again.

Serial entrepreneurship is a great path for multipotentialites who like starting things and sticking with them until they've made an impact. At their cores, serial entrepreneurs are passionate and fiercely independent problem solvers. Tina Roth Eisenberg, also known as swissmiss, is a designer and entrepreneur who has launched four rad companies: a global monthly lecture series called CreativeMornings, a to-do app called TeuxDeux, a "designy" temporary tattoo shop called Tattly, and a coworking space called FRIENDS. Like the Phoenix multipotentialites we met, who establish their new careers before leaving their old ones, Tina is a strong advocate of side projects. All four of her companies began as side projects and organically grew into businesses. Are you a self-starter who always has a project of some sort that you pour yourself into in your spare time? You might just be a serial entrepreneur at heart.

Trying on the Phoenix Approach

Do you do things sequentially, by nature? Do you really like zeroing in on a topic for a while? Let's see what your life might look like if you were to adopt the Phoenix Approach.

WHAT WOULD YOU DO IF YOU HAD MULTIPLE LIVES?

You are magically given ten lives and you can be anything you want in each life. What will you be? Make a list. (You can go higher than ten if you need to.)

IDENTIFY YOUR PRIORITIES

Underline one to three careers on your list that you are itching to explore right now.

BRAINSTORM AND RESEARCH SOME STRATEGIES TO GET IN THE DOOR

For each career that you underlined, ask:

- Do I know anyone who is involved in or connected to this industry?

- Are there any upcoming events in the field that I could attend?

- Where could I volunteer?

- Could I do this in a freelance capacity? If so, is there a small business owner that I would love to do some free work for?

- How much education does this profession require? Is there a class or educational program I could sign up for?

- What skills do I already have that could be useful in this new context?

MAKE A LIST OF POSSIBLE SIDE PROJECTS

On a new page, list any side projects you're currently working on or have been wanting to start. Could any of these projects turn into businesses? Would you want to monetize them?

WHAT PROBLEMS WOULD YOU LIKE TO FIX?

One of the best ways to come up with business ideas is to think about the problems that you or the people around you are facing. If the idea of becoming a serial entrepreneur appeals to you, get yourself a notebook and begin jotting down problems that you notice and potential solutions you come up with.

TAKING ACTION

If you're excited about the idea of being something new every few years, decide on one to three small action steps to take this week to get started. Your action steps will depend on your unique situation, but here are a few possible examples:

- Set an alarm on your phone for the middle of the workday tomorrow. When the alarm goes off, take a minute to notice how you feel in your body. Where are you on the loathing scale?

- Put out a call to your network. Let them know that you're trying to get experience in <insert your new dream field here> and ask whether they have any leads for you.

- Research someone you would like to do free work for and identify one thing they could be doing / doing better that you could help with.

KEY POINTS FROM THIS CHAPTER

The Phoenix work model allows us to balance the desire to go deep and immerse ourselves in an area with the need for diverse experiences. Here's what we covered:

- The Phoenix Approach is working in a single field for several months or years and then shifting gears and starting a new career in a different field.

- This model is a good fit for sequential multipotentialites who like exploring their interests one at a time.

- Phoenix careers don't usually provide much variety, but we can make them more multifaceted by blending the Phoenix Approach with other work models.

- A Phoenix's path may look scattered and random from the outside, but there is often a common Why underlying each career.

- The right time to set the stage for a transition is when you are feeling bored. Don't wait until you are so unhappy that even thinking about work makes you feel ill.

- Aim for a graceful transition by establishing your new career on the side before switching.

- To break into a new industry, try any or all of these: reach out to your existing network, expand your network by meeting new people, volunteer, do free work, get some training, emphasize your transferable skills.

- If you're an independent self-starter, you might consider serial entrepreneurship: the self-employment version of the Phoenix career.

PART III

COMMON MULTIPOTENTIALITE STUMBLING BLOCKS

SLAYING YOUR DRAGONS

Hooray! You know your superpowers, and which approach might be the best way to harness them. You're unstoppable!

Kind of. As you probably know, we humans have a tendency to get in our own way. We are excellent at curbing our efforts, especially if those efforts are deeply important to us. In these next couple chapters, we'll discuss the biggest challenges that we need to deal with to build a life around our many passions: our difficulty with productivity and the specter of multipotentialite insecurities. Don't worry, it's totally possible to overcome these obstacles. We just need the right tools.

8

YOUR PERSONAL PRODUCTIVITY SYSTEM

How does a person focus on several things and make progress on all of them? As multipotentialites, is it even possible to fit every passion into our lives without spinning our wheels or going crazy? And what about the internal *muck* that accompanies our important projects? You know, the procrastination, the self-doubt, the overwhelm, the chronic e-mail checking. . . . How does anyone get anything done, ever?!

Productivity is **taking action that moves us toward our goals**. For many of us, productivity is linked with our happiness and even our sense of self-worth. When our day slips away from us and we have accomplished little, it feels like a defeat. When we can look back on our day and see all that we have accomplished—that we took charge, directed our focus, and made a good dent in an important project—we feel good about ourselves. Productivity as a virtue can certainly be over-emphasized and taken to an unhealthy level. But I'm not ad-vocating for overwork, "busywork," or even efficiency here. This section is about having the agency we need to move our projects forward and to deal with any creative, emotional, and logistical roadblocks that ~~might~~ will arise.

A CUSTOMIZED APPROACH

As long as there have been philosophers and intellectuals, humans have been thinking and writing about how to be more productive. However, most productivity advice isn't formulated with the multipotentialite in mind. It doesn't reflect or consider our need for variety. Specialist-oriented productivity advice usually advocates following a rigid system, and we multipo-tentialites require a flexible approach. Though we need wiggle room pretty much across the board, we all work differently. We are all motivated by different carrots and sticks, if you will. Some of us like to plan out every hour of every week in advance, while others rebel against even the thought of structuring our days. Some of us have trouble getting down to business, while others have a hard time disconnecting and feel guilty for taking time off. As we grow and change, our productivity strategies need to evolve with us. Basically, we each need to design (and sometimes redesign) our own customized productivity system.

Instead of taking a one-size-fits-all approach, we're going to explore a number of individual tools. Some of these tools will speak to you and others won't. Some may need to be cus-tomized, and I encourage you to change them up as you see fit. Experiment, make them your own, and piece together *your* system.

For multipotentialites, productivity is about more than just getting things done. We need to make sure that we're working on the *right things,* that our schedule is conducive to getting things done, and that we understand when it is time to abandon a project and move on to the next. Last but definitely not least, we need to figure out how to focus, take action, and actually make things happen. The tools in this chapter are separated into four broad categories:

- Choosing what to focus on

- Finding the time

- Knowing when to quit

- Getting yourself to do the work

Let's load up a pomodoro[1] and get started!

CHOOSING WHAT TO FOCUS ON

One of the most challenging aspects of being a multipotentialite is figuring out which of our "potentials" to develop. We can do many things, but probably not all at once. And (you may want to sit down for this one) we can't literally do *all the things.* Our time on Earth is finite, after all. However, we can still experience a heck of a lot during a single lifetime! There is a vast, vast middle ground between doing everything under the sun

---

1. This will make sense soon.

and doing just one thing—and that middle ground is where multipotentialites play.

Making choices about what to do first can be terrifying. It's easy to fixate on the idea that taking one path precludes us from taking any others (this is what we've been told all our lives). We sometimes approach new endeavors with a sinking feeling in our gut, knowing that we might later rescind our decision and change directions. *So what's the point of even moving forward with anything?* These fears are enough to paralyze us into inaction. The truth is, choosing *does* limit our options, but not nearly as much as we might think. Choices are rarely permanent or irreversible. In fact, choices are plastic: they can change even as we make them. Sometimes we can choose three things at once![2] What's more, if we lose interest, it will be because we have gotten what we came for and need to make space in our life for new passions and adventures.

You can't know in advance what will happen when you choose to pursue a particular path. You might fall in love with your chosen project for years to come. You might find that your interest dissipates quickly. Maybe this endeavor will introduce you to new subjects that are even more fascinating. The best you can do is listen to your heart and be brave.[3] The good news is that taking action and letting your heart guide you get easier the more you do them. They can even be thrilling!

For now, we need to take the gravity out of choosing, because **not choosing** is a choice too—often one with much

---

2. Three is just an arbitrary number. There are times when we may be able to choose many more things at once, and other times when we may only have room for one thing at a time. It depends on how all-consuming the projects are and what else is going on in our lives.

3. I know, it's annoying advice.

heavier consequences.[4] When you're picking a project to pursue, try not to think of it as some massive commitment. Can you think of it as an exploration, as something you're trying out? Approach your interests with a sense of curiosity and wonder, and remember to have fun!

Choosing Your Cast

It's party time. Let's make some choices. Grab a pen and a piece of paper. We'll start by dividing up the projects that you *could* be spending time on into two categories:

1. **Priority Projects.** In this category, include the things that you are excited about and are actively pursuing. They could be work projects, personal projects, subjects you are studying, skills you are learning, activities you enjoy. They could even be broader goals like improving your health or strengthening your relationship with your partner.

2. **Projects That Are Waiting in the Wings.** In this category include the things that you are excited about but aren't actively pursuing. List anything that you dabble in occasionally, as well as dormant projects and ideas or activities that you haven't yet had a chance to dig into. Again, these could be any sort of work or personal project, subject, activity, or goal. This list can be as long as you like. In fact,

---

4. I don't like fear tactics so I'm putting this in a footnote. At the end of your life, do you want to look back and marvel at all the incredible things you got to experience, or do you want to think about everything you were too afraid to try? Regret is no fun, so let's have fun exploring now.

feel free to put this list aside after you're done with the exercise. Any time something new strikes your fancy, add it.[5]

You'll notice that we only included projects that excite us on either list. We spend time on plenty of other things—obligations, daily routines, less inspiring work, laundry—but our goal at the moment is to help you make progress on the projects that tug at your heartstrings. It is these projects that are at risk of not seeing the light of day. We need to fit them in *around* your obligations, routines, and less inspiring work that can't be immediately eliminated from your life.

Now back to those exciting projects:

- How many priority projects do you currently have in your life? As we know, some people thrive when they have dozens of projects going on at once, while others do much better with a smaller number. A good starting point is to have one to five priority projects at one time.

- How does this number feel to you? Have you been overwhelmed lately? Have you been a little restless and in need of more variety? Do you have the exact right number of active projects in your life right now to make you feel alive and balanced?

- If you think you may have too many priority projects in your life right now, ask yourself if you could move any of them to the wings. If you aren't able to spend less time on any of these projects at the moment, then maybe one will come to a natural end point soon? If

5. I used to refer to this kind of list as a "back-burner list," but that makes it sound as though these projects are dormant and you won't get to them for a while. If your projects are "waiting in the wings," on the other hand, they could spring into action at any time. It's a more comforting (and accurate) metaphor for multipotentialites.

not, make a plan to move some of them over to the wings as soon as possible.

- If you're feeling as though you would like to prioritize more projects right now, take a look at the projects that are waiting in the wings. Pick one from that list that you'd like to put some time and focus into, maybe one that you've already toyed with a little, and run it through this fun flowchart:

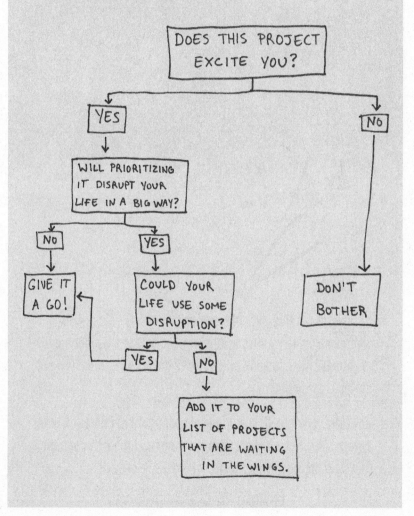

- Once you're satisfied with the number of projects that are on your plate, grab a new sheet of paper. Draw circles for each project. In the center of each circle, describe the project in a few words. Here's an example:

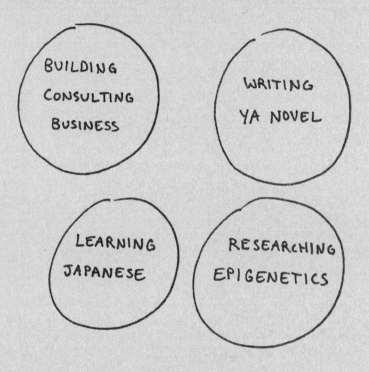

- *Optional:* Hang this piece of paper on the wall by your desk or wherever you do your work. This way you'll have a visual reminder of your priorities so you can easily pick the priority project(s) you'd like to focus on that day.

- Any time you're ready to put one of your priority projects aside for a while, pick a new project from the wings and run it through the flowchart on the previous page.

What If You Are DYING to Work on One of Your Projects That Is Waiting in the Wings?

Another book about productivity might tell you that one to five active projects is plenty to focus on, that you should keep your head down and finish them before spending time on anything else. And this advice might sound totally acceptable to the ears of a specialist. . . . But not to a multipotentialite! We need to be allowed to explore our numerous passions: the niggling subjects that threaten to distract us, the shiny objects and the new fascinations. We may not choose to exercise this freedom, but without the option, we can easily become resentful toward our priority projects. Dabbling in unrelated things can also breathe new life into our work and provide much-needed breaks.

So instead of keeping our eyes fixed resolutely on the stage, let's let them wander a little. Now, if we're going to do this—if we're going to allow ourselves to play with any and every exciting project that is waiting in the wings—then we'd better set some limits for ourselves. We don't want to completely lose track of the play itself, because that would be a big problem, too. We want to balance the need for exploration with the desire for progress.

Dedicated Tinkering Time

Imagine being given a free pass to be utterly and joyfully unproductive for a period of time. You could spend this time exploring something that might or might not lead anywhere, testing out a new idea, dabbling in a new medium, and even multitasking. There is no reason that you can't grant yourself this freedom. Decide on an amount of time that will allow you to have some fun, yet isn't too long. You don't want to become anxious about neglecting your priority projects. Forty minutes is what I recommend, though you may need more or less time depending on the nature of the project(s) and how much time you actually have available. Once you decide on a length of time, set a timer and have at it! You can grant yourself some tinkering time whenever you like, but I recommend doing it later in the day, once you've already gotten a good amount of work done on one or more of your priority projects. You can even treat tinkering time as a reward for all your hard work.

Key Points About Choosing What to Focus On

- Choosing is scary, but choices are rarely permanent and don't limit us nearly as much as we think they will.

- When you pursue an interest, think of it as an exploration rather than a binding contract.

- To help you decide where you should be putting your focus, divide the things you could be focusing on into two categories: your priority projects and your projects that are waiting in the wings.

- Add to your list of projects in the wings when you discover something new to explore.

- When you're ready to retire a priority project, consider replacing it with a project that is waiting in the wings.

- If you are dying to engage with projects that are waiting in the wings, set some dedicated tinkering time. Set a timer so that your tinkering time doesn't take over your entire day. Feel free to multitask, dive into rabbit holes, and otherwise be "unproductive."

FINDING THE TIME

Now that we've made some choices, let's figure out how to fit all our glorious projects into our lives.

When to Work

Everyone has certain times of the day when their mind is at its sharpest and they have the greatest amount of creative energy. We should work on our most important projects during these optimal times. By the same token, there will be times of the day when we are more likely to have low energy and can't get anything done at all. For me, this happens around 4 P.M. I can force it if I have a major deadline coming up or if I just really need to put a dent in something, but my brain is a whole lot slower.

Pay attention to your body. How do you feel throughout the day? Start taking note of your creative and energetic rhythms. When do you feel most excited? When do you feel brain-dead? Are there particular types of activities that you like to do at different times? Maybe creative work is best done in the morning and administrative or collaborative work flows better in the afternoon. Or maybe you like to stay up late and descend into your projects once everyone else has gone to bed.

A quick word of warning: I am not advocating that you wait for inspiration to hit before working on your projects, just that you identify the times of day when you tend to be sharpest and try to align them with your work. The key to creativity (and to making progress on your projects) is to see it as a practice. That is, something that we do on a regular basis, for its own sake. Moments of divine inspiration *do* happen, but usually only if you are already working on something regularly. Waiting for the inspiration to hit is often just Resistance in disguise. We'll talk about strategies to defeat the scary Resistance Monster later in this chapter.

What About Busy or Inflexible Schedules?

In an ideal world, we would be able to align our work times with our energetic and creative rhythms every day. In reality, most of us lead busy lives. We have obligations that we just can't neglect, and relationships we wish to nourish. We aren't always able to work on our projects at the times when we feel most energized. If our schedule doesn't allow us to work at optimal times (or provide us with much time at all), then when should we work on our priority projects? The answer is: *whenever we can.*[6]

Lori Stalter, an accountant-turned-architectural-drafter-turned-business-owner, built her business on her lunch hours. She left her office every day at noon, drove to a nearby park, sat in her car and worked away. Mike Pumphrey, an Einsteiner with

---

6. This same advice applies for people who are struggling with health issues or are going through challenging emotional periods: work when you feel up to it. And in these cases, especially, try not to be hard on yourself for not being "more productive."

a good enough job, has been working on his personal finance blog every Saturday morning for the last four years! He gets up in the morning, goes to a particular café he likes, and spends a few hours working on his blog posts and his newsletter for the week. It's his weekly ritual. Other people who are struggling to make headway on their projects commit to waking up early or staying up for an hour or two after everyone has gone to bed. It's not ideal, but it may be the best you can do for now.[7]

One of the goals of this book is to help you design a more integrated work life, so that you get to tap into your multipotentialite superpowers and eliminate as much bland, disheartening work as possible. This process takes time and experimentation, and sometimes requires a few escapes and transitions. Try to work on your priority projects at the times when you have the most creative energy, but if you have to compromise and work at some less-than-ideal times, then do it. Create rituals for yourself, like Lori and Mike, and use the time you carve out to really go hard on your projects.

Structuring Your Time

There are many ways to structure your time so that you make progress on your priority projects. Your chosen method will depend on several factors, including how busy you are, how flexible your schedule is, your energy levels throughout the day, the nature of your projects, and how deep you like to go.

7. I have noticed an interesting phenomenon among many of my friends who finally quit their jobs to pursue the thing(s) they love. Before quitting, they make use of any and every available moment to work on their projects. But once they quit, they find themselves lost in a sea of newfound free time. The whole day is available to them and they end up squandering the hours and being far less productive. These friends eventually learn how to create boundaries for themselves, but it's an interesting lesson.

Here are some common methods that multipotentialites use to structure their time. As always, feel free to combine or modify these tools as you please.

The Fluid Schedule

Some multipotentialites have trouble sticking to a schedule that is too rigid. Enter the Fluid Schedule. It's an intuitive approach to productivity, and it's held together by the ability to focus on one project at a time. Here's how it works.

Let's say you have some free time right now to work on your priority projects. Great! Maybe you have half an hour, maybe you have four hours, or maybe you have an entire day. Regardless of how much time you have available to you, begin by taking account of your priority projects. If you've hung them on your wall, just look up. Which of these projects would you like to work on right now? You might think about which project:

- You're most in the mood for

- Is most urgent

- Requires attention, for whatever reason

Once you've made your choice, begin! Work on this project and this project only (don't multitask) until you lose steam, finish the task you were working on, or run out of time.

At this point you can:

- Take a break and return to the same project

- Stop entirely

- Switch to another priority project (you can, of course, take a break before you switch)

That's it. Every time you're working on a project and begin to lose steam, take a break and continue, stop, or switch to a new priority project. You can also take some tinkering time, if you are really itching to play with one of your projects that is waiting in the wings.

The Prepared Schedule

Some multipotentialites like planning out our schedules in advance, in varying degrees of detail. *All* of us have times in our lives when we could benefit from a little extra structure. I typically maintain a fluid schedule, but when I'm dealing with a lot of demands or deadlines, I sometimes draw up a schedule for the day or week. By making a prepared schedule, you can allocate time in advance to particular projects, allowing you to feel more confident that the work will actually happen.

Some multipotentialites like to create a regular schedule to use every day. One fun way to do this is to use Barbara Sher's "School Day Life Design Model." In this model, you structure your day the way a student might, going to different classes at different times—only each "class" is a different project. For example:

9 A.M.–11 A.M.: Writing YA novel

11 A.M.–3 P.M.: Building consulting business

3 P.M.–3:40 P.M.: Tinkering time

Evenings: Learning Japanese

Feel free to play with the length of your "periods," as well as the number of projects you include in your schedule. Finally! A school schedule that is totally on your terms.

Project Immersion

Every year, hundreds of thousands of people from around the world write fifty-thousand-word novels in the month of November. It is National Novel Writing Month (or NaNoWriMo), and it is an opportunity to *finally* get that novel you have inside of you out, and do it alongside a supportive community. My friend Rena Hundert and I were inspired by this idea and decided to try it out in a different realm. We used to play music together in college and had always wanted to write an album together. Nearly ten years had passed since college, and life had gotten in the way. We were busy with other projects (she's a comedian and improviser) and had moved to opposite sides of the continent. And yet neither of us could let go of this idea. One day when I was back in Montreal visiting family, Rena and I made the decision to carve out a month (about six months in the future) and to spend that month writing and recording an album together.[8] We have done this twice in the last three years, in different cities, and it is always an intense and joyous experience. Neither of us wants to play in a band full-time, but we both want to have the *experience* of being in a band *a little bit,* on occasion. The monthlong, intensive format gives us that experience. The fact that writing an album is an activity with a specific deliverable and that we give ourselves a one-month deadline helps keep us on track, too.

You don't need to do anything as intense as writing an album or a novel in a month to benefit from the immersive approach. Dedicating a period of time—a month, a week, or even a

---

8. It ended up being a five-song EP, but regardless of length, completing a record was a proud moment for us!

weekend—to a single project is a powerful way to make real progress.

Extended Project Immersion

As we saw in Chapter 7, some multipotentialites become absorbed in a single field or project for a number of months or years before switching to a new domain. This approach isn't for everyone, but some people swear by six-month contracts, or four-year cycles. If you are on the sequential end of the spectrum, you may not need to schedule out every day. Your ideal work setup might be as simple as working on your one priority project until you reach your personal end point.

Key Points About Finding the Time

- Try to work on your priority projects during the times of day when you have the most creative energy.

- If your schedule doesn't allow for this, work whenever you can. Get up early, stay up late, and use your lunch hours and weekends.

- There are many ways to structure your work time. Some multipotentialites take a fluid approach to our schedules, while others prefer planning our schedules out in advance.

- Occasionally immersing ourselves in a single project for a period of time can be an effective way to put a dent in a project.

- If you are more sequential in nature, you might benefit from *not* scheduling out your day, but instead focusing entirely on your one priority project.

Knowing When To Quit

The word *quitter* has a terrible rap. Quitters are seen as weak people, who give up when things get hard. Contrary to popular belief, multipotentialites don't quit when something becomes too difficult; we usually quit because something has become *too easy*. Once we're no longer challenged, we lose interest and we want to explore a new area.

What looks like quitting from the outside might actually be the finish line for a multipotentialite. As Barbara Sher explains, scanners (a.k.a. multipotentialites) define finishing differently than most people. To most, finishing means hitting an external end point, like obtaining a degree or devoting your life to one path. It is the "till death do us part" (or at least "till retirement do us part") definition of finishing. **Multipotentialites, on the other hand, are finished once we get what we came for.** According to Barbara,

> When you lose interest in something, you must always consider the possibility that you've gotten what you came for; you have completed your mission. [. . .] That's why you lose interest: not because you're flawed or lazy or unable to focus, but because you're finished.

The Personal End Point

You have reached your Personal End Point once you have gotten what you came for. "What you came for" could be the completion of a project or it could be something more personal like acquiring a skill, feeling a sense of mastery, or expressing yourself creatively. I once had a student who told me she loves understanding the "syntax" behind her various interests. She enjoys diving in, cracking the code, and understanding how something works—the hidden pattern, language, and scripts that are at play. Once she understands that syntax, she gets bored. At this point, she has reached her Personal End Point. Another way to figure out when you've reached the end is to think about your Why(s). If you lose interest, then there's a good chance that whatever it was that drove you to this subject in the first place is exactly what you've experienced or achieved and you are ready to move on.

Your Personal End Point vs. Resistance

As you near your Personal End Point, you're likely to begin feeling bored. Boredom is your mind's way of letting you know that it's time to move on. However, there is another force that can cause remarkably similar symptoms of boredom and dread: Resistance. Resistance is a force within us that wants to keep us safe. It tries to prevent us from shaking things up, pushing ourselves, and taking risks (even creative risks). Resistance has noble intentions, but it can really get in the way of our ability to take action. As author and historian Steven Pressfield explains in his book *The War of Art,* Resistance can take various forms including fear, self-sabotage, procrastination, and self-loathing. And "[t]he more important a call or action is to our soul's evolution, the more Resistance we will feel toward pursuing it."

Let's say you begin to feel unchallenged or uninspired by a project that you've been working on. How do you know whether you've reached your Personal End Point or whether the scary Resistance Monster is simply doing everything it can to prevent you from working on this deeply important project?

The secret to differentiating between these two forces is to pay attention to how you feel physically and emotionally. Resistance and a Personal End Point feel different in your body. Resistance usually comes on fast and is very intense. It makes you want to quit instantly. Your Personal End Point, on the other hand, is usually a growing awareness that you've learned or accomplished all you need to in an area, that you're *basically done here*. This restlessness comes on slowly and the reality that we're ready to move on is often something we try to ignore. Resistance is impossible to ignore. Resistance often brings with it fear, self-doubt, and anxiety, and yet, excitement and passion still lurk beneath the surface. When you reach your Personal End Point, you might feel fear (fear often accompanies change), but excitement and passion for your project have usually faded.

Here are a few clues to help you differentiate a Personal End Point from Resistance:

- Do you feel a sense of excitement in addition to your boredom? Or is it really just boredom?

- Do you feel panicky about your project, or is it more of a dull aching feeling?

- Did the desire to quit creep up on you slowly or hit like a tidal wave?

- Are you feeling insecure about yourself or your ability in regard to this project?

- How challenging is this project and how challenging was it when you began? Are you struggling right now, or has it gotten easier (maybe too easy)?

If you feel some excitement and panic, the desire to quit came on suddenly, you're feeling insecure, and/or your project is challenging right now, then there's a good chance that what you're dealing with is Resistance. Hold on and keep moving forward with your project. If the feeling persists steadily[9] for much longer, you can always reassess.

Key Points About Knowing When to Quit

- Multipotentialites don't quit when something becomes too hard; we quit because something has become *too easy*.

- To most people, finishing means hitting an external end point. Multipotentialites, on the other hand, are finished once we get what we came for.

- Once you have gotten what you came for you have reached your Personal End Point.

- Resistance is the force within us that tries to keep things as they are. It can cause us to procrastinate or self-sabotage.

- It's easy to confuse Resistance with a Personal End Point. They both produce feelings of boredom, dread, restlessness, and fear.

9. Keep in mind that Resistance never really goes away. It can subside, but it has a pesky tendency to pop up from time to time, especially when we're doing important, juicy stuff like pushing ourselves outside our comfort zones.

- The way to determine whether you're dealing with Resistance or a Personal End Point is to pay attention to how you're feeling in your body. With time, you will learn to identify the signs, so you can decide whether to stick with a project or move on to a new adventure.

GETTING YOURSELF TO DO THE WORK

There is a big difference between knowing what you should be working on and actually *getting down to work*. The latter can be challenging, almost excruciating at times. It can feel like you literally need to trick yourself into working on the projects that matter to you most. Here are some tools to help you make consistent progress on your priority projects. These techniques are also good antidotes to Resistance.

Get Yourself into a Positive Emotional State Before Working

Sometimes, you wake up bright-eyed and bushy-tailed, raring to go on a particular project. Other times, you wake without any momentum at all. You know that day, several months into a project, when you realize that you no longer want to leap to your desk with excitement? It doesn't necessarily mean that you aren't eager to continue or that you've fallen out of love with your project. It might mean that it's time to create a little *intentional inspiration* for yourself.

For better or worse, the things we do shape our moods. In particular, routines and rituals can give us a kind of reflexive inspiration, if they are linked in our mind with our creativity. Some people use a specific morning routine to get in the mind-set to create. Others have rituals they do just prior to working, regardless of the time of day. Here are a few tools that you can try individually or in combination, as part of a prework ritual:

- *Meditation:* If you haven't meditated before, start by setting a timer for just five minutes. Isolate a physical feeling to focus on. This feeling could be the rising and falling sensation of your breath in your body or the physical sensation of each part of your body as you scan from head to toe. When a thought arises, acknowledge the thought and then redirect your focus back to whatever physical sensation you're focusing on. I recommend using a guided meditation tool like an audio recording or meditation app when you are first getting started.[10]

- *Movement:* Exercise increases blood flow and oxygen to the brain, making it easier to focus. Get out of your head and into your body with some physical activity. You can make this as intense or as leisurely as you please. Walk, run, swim, exercise, bike, do yoga—whatever works for you. Bonus: You'll be tired so sitting your butt in a chair (if that's what your work requires) will be a treat, not a chore!

- *Gratitude:* Gratitude, as a practice, has gotten a lot of attention recently and has become a bit of a buzzword.

10. I like the Headspace app.

But there is good reason that so many people are talking about gratitude: thinking about what you're grateful for actually does put you in a better mood. Think about ten things you are grateful for. Even better: think of ways you're grateful with regard to your projects/passions/ careers. Don't just list them off; actually take some time and try to *feel* the emotion.

- *Visualization:* Think about each of your priority projects one at a time. Don't go over all the tasks you need to accomplish. Instead, focus on the big picture. If you are building a T-shirt business, imagine how you will feel on the day you launch or make your first sale. If you are writing a novel, picture someone reading your book and being deeply moved. You can also grab your Perfect Day exercise from Chapter 3, and imagine how it will feel to live out this day.

- *Setting up your environment:* Do whatever you need to do to make your environment conducive to creativity. You might clear off your desk, lay out and organize your materials, light a candle, or otherwise cozy up your space.

What's the Next Itty-Bitty Step?

It's easy to get overwhelmed when thinking about *everything* you need to do in your projects. Instead of focusing on the big picture, shift your gaze to the immediate next step. Imagine you are driving a car from one end of a country to the other at night. The car lights don't have to light up the whole route for you to get there. You just need to see about two hundred feet into the darkness to move forward. Which one to three itty-bitty action steps can you take right now to move your project forward?

Set a Timer

The timer is probably the most underrated productivity tool. Here are a few good ways to make use of a timer:

- *The Pomodoro Technique:* This technique was developed by author and entrepreneur Francesco Cirillo in the early 1990s. Cirillo used a tomato-shaped kitchen timer, hence the name "Pomodoro." The method works by breaking up your projects into short sprints, which makes you less likely to get distracted. Here's how to do it:

  1. Set a timer for twenty-five minutes and spend this time working on a single project. You've just completed one pomodoro.

  2. Take a five-minute break.

  3. Repeat steps one and two. When you've completed four pomodoros, take a twenty-five-minute break.

  That's it. You can make your pomodoros longer or shorter, or modify the structure to suit your needs. Sometimes I'll start a work session by using the Pomodoro Technique and then after a few pomodoros, I'll transition into a longer period of sustained focus and lose the timer.

- *Go Nuts for Five Minutes:* If you're having a hard time getting started, set a timer for five minutes and work like craaazzzzzzzy on one of your projects. Really go hard. At the end of the five minutes, allow yourself to stop. You will often find that, once you break the ice, you'll want to keep going. (But if you do stop, that's okay.)

- *The "Whichever Happens First" Technique:* Set a timer for a certain amount of time and tell yourself that you can stop working once you complete a specific task or the timer goes off, whichever happens first. I used this technique when I was in law school and trying to write a television script at the same time. Every day I set a timer for forty minutes and told myself that I could stop working on my script once the timer went off or I finished a scene, whichever happened first.

- *Just Set a Timer:* This doesn't need to be complicated. It almost doesn't matter how long you set your timer for. Simply setting one is often enough to propel you into action.

Induce a Flow State

Have you ever been so immersed in a project that the whole world seemed to dissolve, leaving only you and your work? You felt happy, brilliant, and calm. The work streaming out of you was so inspired, it was as if the creative gods were speaking through you. Perhaps you eventually looked up at the clock and were shocked to find that only twenty minutes had gone by, or conversely maybe hours had zipped by in a flash. The state I'm describing is what psychologist Mihaly Csikszentmihalyi refers to as *flow*. He describes flow in his book *Flow: The Psychology of Optimal Experience* as "the mental state of operation in which a person performing an activity is fully immersed in a feeling of energized focus, full involvement, and enjoyment in the process of the activity." In short, we are at our happiest and most productive when we're in a flow state.

Multipotentialites want to investigate, do, and be everything. But our time is limited. Learning how to induce (or at least encourage) a flow state at will is a huge asset. I should say, flow states are sometimes effortless and other times quite elusive. When you find yourself in a flow state, pay attention. What kind of habits, rituals, and environments got you there? Over time, these elements can become cues for your brain that it's time to get to work. Personally, I can't help but be superproductive at a coffee shop in the morning with a hot cup of tea. And if I need an extra boost, having earbuds in my ears (without music) does it. Weird, huh?

Watch Your Three "C"s

I first learned about the "three 'C's" in Leo Babauta's book *Focus,* and it's a concept that I return to frequently. The principle goes like this: the majority of our activities can be divided into three categories: *creating, connecting,* and *consuming.* Creating involves bringing something new into existence. Connecting involves reaching out to others and can include activities such as responding to e-mails or posting on social media. Consuming is any activity that involves research or learning. It can consist of reading books or articles, watching movies, listening to podcasts, and so on. All three categories of activities are important. But to get the most out of them, you should respect the combining rule: ***Connecting and Consuming activities can be combined, but should never be combined with Creating.*** This means that you can check your e-mail, read your favorite blogs, listen to podcasts, and flip between books all at the same time, if you like. However, it's not effective to combine any of these activities with acts of Creating. Just create.

SPECIAL TOOLS FOR ZERO-PROGRESS DAYS

Some days, we just have a hard time getting started. Here are a few bonus strategies to help you out when you're having a rough time getting anything done.

Lower Your Expectations

Many of us have a tendency to write up intimidatingly long to-do lists for ourselves each morning. When we fall short, these lengthy documents can leave us feeling terrible about ourselves. As author Chris Guillebeau points out, "[w]e overestimate what we can accomplish in a day, but underestimate what we can accomplish in a year." Instead of writing out a thousand things that you want to finish up that day, make an agreement with yourself that if you get a nice chunk of work done on *one* of your priority projects, you will be done. Once you finish you can, of course, keep going. But the rest is bonus work—and go you!

Track Your Small Wins

We are excellent at seeing all the places we've fallen short, the work that didn't get done, and the things that went wrong. We're far less good at noticing what *did* work. We're sometimes even downright afraid to take stock of our wins for fear that appreciating them will, in itself, make them vanish.

There is an evolutionary reason for this. We are wired to notice the negative more than the positive.[11] Think about it: if you're always looking for potential problems, you will notice that lion lurking in the forest or stock up on food before a storm hits. The problem is that, much like the Resistance Monster, this evolution-mediated response is often misplaced in the creative realm. The ability to focus on the negative is not much help when you are trying to pursue a new project. Negativity slows us down and makes us feel bad about our progress and ourselves (because all we see is how little we accomplished). It prevents us from appreciating and enjoying our work.

Tracking your small wins is a powerful way to combat the natural tendency toward negativity. Here's how it works:

- Get a journal. I recommend a small journal so that the pages are easier to fill and you'll be less likely to notice the white space. This is your official "small wins journal." Use it for nothing else. Guard it with your life.[12]

- Jot down your small wins whenever they happen or at the end of each work session.

11. In scientific terms, this is called "negativity bias."
12. Just kidding. Sharing your wins is awesome.

- Focus on logging actions that *you* take rather than the responses or results you get from other people. For instance, it's better to write, "I pitched an article to a magazine," than "My article was accepted by a magazine," because this way you are noting *your action* and seeing *that* as the important factor. You can't control other people's reactions but you can control what you do. If your action alone is a win, then you will take even more action and get more and better results.

- Of course, you can also track the wins that come as a result of other people's actions. It's just that you shouldn't wait for them before logging a win. So write, "Launched my first product!" first and then you can add, "Made a bunch of sales!" later.

- No win is too small. This is called a small wins journal for a reason. If you feel like you didn't accomplish anything that day, challenge yourself by saying the following sentence out loud: *Okay, so I feel like I didn't get anything done today. . . . But if I had to come up with three small wins, what would they be?* It's really okay if your wins are minuscule at first or they don't feel like wins to you at all. So you didn't hit your thousand-word goal for the short story you're writing. Did you write a page? Half a page? Great, mark that down. Did you practice the guitar for ten minutes? That's another win. If you track your small wins, they will eventually start growing and you'll be able to look back and see how far you've come.

- The best time to track your small wins is when you begin exploring a brand-new subject. In the early stages, it's common to feel awkward about your lack of skill or discouraged by the heaps of work ahead of you. Noticing and celebrating some small wins can really help keep your spirits up so that you continue moving forward.

Get an Accountability Buddy

Everything gets easier when you aren't going it alone. Find a supportive friend who is pursuing their own projects or goals. Get together every couple of weeks to talk about how your projects are progressing and brainstorm any issues that have come up since you last spoke. At the end of each meeting, set some goals for yourselves. Make these goals manageable, and tell each other when you will complete them. When your friend hits their goals, cheer them on. And if they fall short, don't give them too hard a time. You'll probably find that committing to something in front of your accountability buddy is enough to motivate you to actually get it done. Do you know anyone who would make a good accountability buddy? Spend five to ten minutes brainstorming and jot down a few names of people to reach out to.

IF ALL ELSE FAILS . . .

Most of the tools in this chapter can be used to combat the irritating Resistance Monster. Here are a few extra things to try when you're really feeling stuck.

Release Your Feelings

If you're dealing with a lot of Resistance, you probably have some pretty intense emotions brewing under the surface. You might be feeling afraid, angry, upset, worried, anxious, irritated, sad, or all of the above. Get these emotions out. You can do this by:

- Throwing a tantrum. I'm not kidding, this is allowed. Find a place where you can be alone (you might warn any unsuspecting family members or roommates nearby) and then do whatever you need to do: yell, stomp, punch a pillow, curse the world. Make it dramatic! You will probably find that after a few minutes of this, your intense emotions begin to subside. You might even start laughing at the sheer absurdity of what not-being-able-to-write-that-poem has turned you into.

- Journal. Free write. Don't censor yourself.[13]

Take a Break

If work just isn't happening, it's okay to take a break. Go for a walk, get out of the house, move your body. You can also take some tinkering time and "cheat" on your priority projects with your other, "less serious" work. And of course, you're welcome to take a full-on break and just do nothing. Naps are fantastic, as are movies. Any break activity is fair game as long as it helps you get out of your head and recharge.

13. And don't use your small wins journal for this!

TAKING ACTION

It's time to put together your very own personal productivity system. Take a look back over this chapter and pick out five techniques to try. Behold your handy productivity toolkit! When you're gearing up to work or find yourself feeling stuck, come back to these techniques and give them a go. Modify them as needed or swap them out for other tools in this chapter if they aren't working for you. Different strategies work for different people, so experiment and make these your own.

FEAR, CONFIDENCE, AND DEALING WITH PEOPLE WHO DON'T UNDERSTAND

What really holds multipotentialites back? What gets in the way of us tapping into our superpowers, exploring the nooks and crannies of our interests, and bringing our marvelous projects to life? One obstacle is a lack of career resources. We aren't taught the mechanics of how multipotentialites build sustainable, multifaceted careers. Another obstacle is scheduling and logistics: that irritating issue of *time*. But the third, most subtle and often most stifling challenge for multipotentialites is the self-doubt we sometimes experience living in a world that doesn't recognize our strengths (or even our existence). We can be our own worst enemies. We put our ideas down. We second-guess ourselves. We let the fear of being judged keep us stuck in careers that no longer serve us and identities that no longer fit.

Maybe you grew up in an environment where your multipotentiality was nurtured and celebrated, or maybe you had an opposite experience. Perhaps you faced (or still face) tremendous pressure from your family to specialize in a single field. Even if the people in your life didn't pressure you to pick a single path, those pressures are everywhere in our culture and most of us have internalized this message to some degree. These beliefs can be more harmful than "real" obstacles like time and money. In this chapter, we're going to look at the most pervasive multipotentialite insecurities and discuss strategies for addressing the internal and external critics that threaten to hold us back from embracing our plurality. Make sure to come back to this down the line, whenever you're facing these doubts and anxieties, as that's when the messages will really resonate.

THE CALL IS COMING FROM INSIDE THE HOUSE!

The voices inside us are often the cruelest. Hopefully, figuring out you're a multipotentialite has helped silence some of the self-doubt and unkind self-talk that may have been there before. But it is normal for long-standing insecurities to occasionally rear their heads even if we've embraced our multipotentiality for a long while. Let's go over a few of the most common multi-potentialite "ailments" and come up with some ways of responding to our pesky internal critic.

MULTIPOTENTIALITE AILMENT #1: GUILT AND SHAME

It can be crushing to realize that you've reached your Personal End Point in something you once loved. You may have invested countless hours, sweat, tears, and money into this thing. Maybe you even thought it was The Thing. When you lose interest, you're left with a painful realization that You Were Wrong.

I've been here many times. I lost interest in music in my early twenties and felt completely lost: *Without music, who am I? Everyone knows me as a musician. I view myself as a musician. How could I have lost interest in music? I don't know who I am anymore!* I experienced similar feelings when my interest in film faded, and when I got bored with law. . . . Going through these emotions, you will worry that you've failed yourself and you might feel profoundly lost, guilty, and ashamed. You'll also mourn the good times you had and the passion that is no longer there.

How to Address These Insecurities

Here are a few things to remember when you're going through the shame, guilt, and the existential angst of losing interest in something you once loved:

1. ***You are a multipotentialite, so these shifts in direction
   make complete sense.*** You don't need to feel guilty for
   moving on, because moving on is what multipotentialites
   do. Remaining in a field out of guilt is like staying in a
   relationship with someone you no longer love because
   you're afraid of hurting them. Unlike in a relationship,
   however, the only person you're hurting here is yourself.[1]

2. ***There's more excitement to come.*** Letting something
   go frees you up so that you can move on to your next
   wonderful adventure. There, you will acquire new skills
   and you'll take these skills with you into every new
   realm you explore. Your life will be more interesting for
   it and you'll meet all kinds of amazing people because
   you didn't let yourself remain stuck in a field you've
   outgrown.

3. ***You are not what you do.*** Changes don't have to shatter
   your sense of identity. You are not your medium. ***You are
   not your job.*** You are bigger than "musician" or "teacher"
   or "electrical engineer." You are whole, regardless of your
   title (or even without one at all).

4. ***Adjust your expectations.*** From now on, try to embark
   on new pursuits with appropriate expectations. You
   know that you are a multipotentialite, so don't approach
   a new interest with a "this is it!" mentality. It is more
   constructive to say to yourself that you're going to "try
   something on" for a while and see where it takes you.

1. Actually, that's not completely true. You're also hurting the people you will
potentially touch in your next endeavor by depriving them of your ideas,
skills, and presence.

As you become more comfortable with your mutable nature, you'll start to see transitions as exciting and necessary rather than shameful, identity-crushing events. You'll realize that everything you've experienced, created, and learned is still with you, fortifying your ability to enter new realms with a more complex and nuanced perspective.

MULTIPOTENTIALITE AILMENT #2: THE DISCOMFORT OF BEING A BEGINNER AGAIN AND AGAIN

Multipotentialites are often beginners. In fact, beginnerdom pretty much comes with the territory of wanting to do and be many different things. Many of us love learning—we might even be quite adept learners—but even the most self-assured multipotentialite can feel vulnerable and uncomfortable in the early stages of a new pursuit. Starting something new is uncomfortable. It's easy to wish we could hit the fast-forward button and move on to the part where we have at least some semblance of competence!

How to Address This Insecurity

Here are a few things you can do to lessen the discomfort of those early learning curves:

1. *Realize mediocrity is a necessary first step.* Being bad at something is a necessary part of the process of

becoming good (and then great) at it.[2] That might seem obvious, but it's easy to forget that incompetence is a required step. It's easy to prematurely declare yourself to be "bad at drawing," or "bad at science." You might just need more time. As Jake the Dog from *Adventure Time* says: "Sucking at something is the first step to becoming sorta good at something."

2. ***Keep track of your small wins.*** In the previous chapter we talked about how motivational it can be to notice and celebrate your small wins by tracking them in a journal. This is especially true when you're learning something. Every time you grasp a concept or make even a modicum of progress, write it down. Tracking your small wins will help lift your spirits and keep you motivated so that you can continue learning.

3. ***Work for shorter increments, more frequently.*** Working for shorter periods of time, more frequently, will help new information sink in your brain and muscle memory faster. Shorter work periods also prevent you from getting too frustrated. When my dog, Grendel, was just a little puppy, she very much wanted to respond to my commands, but her brain just couldn't figure out what "down" and "stay" meant. If we worked on training for too long, she would become frustrated and distracted and give up. So we worked in five- to ten-minute increments, once or twice a day (with plenty of treats) and eventually she got it.

2. Check out Anne Lamott's "Shitty First Drafts" idea in her delightful book, *Bird by Bird*, for some therapeutic backup.

4. ***Be kind to yourself.*** Speaking of treats, another lesson I learned from dog training is that positive reinforcement is far more effective than scolding. Now that I think about it, we could all learn a lot from dog training. Treat yourself like a confused but well-meaning little creature. Be gentle, be patient, celebrate your small wins, try to avoid putting yourself down, and eat a cookie from time to time.

MULTIPOTENTIALITE AILMENT #3: THE FEAR OF NOT BEING THE BEST

One of the most common concerns for multipotentialites is that we won't measure up to specialists who have been working in a field for decades. This inner voice sounds like:

- *Why would someone hire me, a former chef, as a project manager when they could hire someone who has been in the industry for years?*

- *Why would anyone want to work with a health practitioner who is also a professional dancer, when they could find a doctor who has been obsessed with medicine since the age of five?*

How to Address This Insecurity

We already know that multipotentialites offer incredible and unique value.[3] We know that multipotentialites possess super-

3. See Chapter 2.

powers and are often well compensated for our creativity and for our unique mélange of skills. So what are some comebacks for those times when you're worrying about whether or not you measure up?

1. ***Being effective matters more than being the best.*** Are your clients happy with your work? Is your boss delighted? Well then, you've done your job. Your work should be about delivering, not about reaching the top of your field.[4] Don't worry about what other people are doing. Focus on bringing your all and making your audience— whoever that may be—really happy.

2. ***It's impossible to actually be the best.*** Even if you dedicate your life to one discipline, you will likely never reach number one. There will always be someone more skilled and someone less skilled than you—that's just life. Pursuing something with the goal of being better than everyone else pits you against other people and creates an atmosphere where you're constantly comparing yourself to others and judging yourself. It's also kind of a narcissistic trap, when you think about it. It is much more helpful to focus on developing your proficiency to the extent that it's professionally useful or personally meaningful.

3. ***This might be a branding issue.*** If you find that people are choosing specialists over you despite the fact that you can do the work just as well, you might not be explaining your value effectively. Whether you're in a job

---

4. It's okay to care about moving up in the ranks, but the quality of your work should be your first priority. And anyway, overdelivering might actually be your way up.

interview or writing copy for your website, focus on how you will solve clients' problems, on what you can do for them. Explain how the different parts of your eclectic background make you better at the job at hand. Stress your transferable skills. Perhaps working at a day care taught you about wrangling groups and keeping their attention, and this skill will make you a better tour guide. Or maybe you learned how to take a complicated issue and distill it down to a digestible article when you were a journalist, and this means you will be great at writing snappy social media updates. Make those connections explicit and frame your value as it relates to the needs of the person you're trying to impress.

4. ***You're an expert until someone says otherwise—and they usually don't.*** Here's a little secret: there's no National Guild of Experts out there, giving out badges to the true masters and exposing the amateurs as fakes. The fact is that most potential employers and clients are looking for people who understand their particular problem and can provide them with solutions. If you present yourself with confidence and link your skills to concrete results, the right people will want to work with you.

MULTIPOTENTIALITE AILMENT #4: IMPOSTER SYNDROME

Imposter syndrome is a belief that deep down, you are a fraud, that you shouldn't be here, and that one day everyone will wake up and realize it. The funny thing about imposter syndrome is that it tends to get worse, not better, as bigger opportunities and successes come our way. When my TED talk was featured on TED.com, I was elated. In the weeks that followed, I received accolades and heartfelt thank-yous—incredible e-mails and messages from all over the world. And all I wanted to do was hide under my bed. *They all think I'm so smart, but what if my ideas are utter garbage?! What if I'm a big fat phony?! I don't even have any credentials!!!* Over time, as I began to see the impact my work was having on people's lives and I focused on new work projects, I started to believe in myself again. But you better believe that imposter syndrome has come up again for me—maybe even during the writing of this book.[5] *What if the publisher was wrong about me and they think this manu- script is terrible and demand that I return my advance?!!* You get the idea.

How to Address This Insecurity

Here are a few ways to deal with the disheartening fantasy of imposter syndrome:

1. ***If you were actually an imposter, you wouldn't get imposter syndrome.*** Imposters are liars, bent on tricking others and profiting from that deceit. I'm pretty sure you aren't one. You aren't trying to deceive anyone. You're just trying to do good work, and the effort to create something new ~~sometimes~~ always inspires uncertainty. Philosopher Bertrand Russell once wrote, "The trouble with the world is that the stupid are cocksure and the intelligent are full

---

5. Wink wink, nudge nudge.

of doubt." *If you occasionally doubt yourself, take it as a sign that you're one of the good ones.*

2. *Refocus on the work itself.* Imposter syndrome usually arises when we become preoccupied with what others might be thinking or saying about us. Instead of focusing on how you are perceived, get back to work. Show yourself through your own actions that you know what you're doing. Turn the negativity and fear in your head into action.

3. *Everyone feels this way sometimes.* Well, okay, not everyone. As we just discussed, con artists probably don't experience imposter syndrome. But every well-meaning person who is pursuing something that matters to them feels as though they don't belong some of the time. As the saying goes, try not to compare your insides to other people's outsides. If you're standing in a room full of colleagues, I guarantee you that you aren't the only one feeling like there's been a big mistake and you actually shouldn't be there.

FACING YOUR EXTERNAL CRITICS

Multipotentialite insecurities don't always originate from within. Sometimes our anxieties come about in reaction to an outside voice: a concerned parent, a confused colleague, an arrogant teacher. . . . Every multipotentialite knows how it feels to share a new interest with someone and receive a blank stare or look of disapproval:

- *"You're going to school to become a sports therapist? But I thought you were happy working at that tech company? That seemed like a good job."*

- *"You're an arts major, so why on earth would you want to take a math class?"*[6]

- *"Would you stop messing around with all of these different ideas and commit to something already?"*

Negative responses to our plurality range from the genuinely confused but well meaning to the outright nasty and critical. Let's discuss some strategies for dealing with the people in our lives who don't understand or approve of our multipotentiality.

Who Is Your Audience?

First, ask yourself who this "critic" is. Is the person a close friend or family member, a casual acquaintance, or someone you know professionally? How much do you care about your relationship with them? Is it a positive force in your life? If the disapproving party is a parent, close friend, or someone whose relationship you value, it's worth trying to help them understand what's going on with you. If they are a passing acquaintance or someone you don't care for, it might be easier (and more pleasant) *not* to explain yourself or seek their approval.

Come Out About Being a Multipotentialite

If you decide that the person is worth your time, try helping them understand what it means to be a multipotentialite. Explain to them that exploring many different subjects and having a lot

6. True story.

of different projects is *who you are.* This way, they won't be so confused the next time you embark on something new. Maybe they'll even ask you what neat things you've been up to. If you want to explain what it means to be a multipotentialite, but don't feel like you have the words or want to engage directly, you can point them to resources about multipotentialites such as books, articles, or TED talks.[7]

Convey Confidence

You can talk about your multipotentiality in many ways. One is to stammer, shrug, and (in an apologetic tone) say something like: "Um, I'm doing this . . . Oh, and also that . . . And, yeah, this other thing. . . ." Another way is to share your enthusiasm for your projects and speak with confidence:[8] "Well, right now I'm involved in _____ . (Full stop.) I'm also *so* excited about _____ ! And when I have a free moment I've been getting up to _____ ." Try to avoid qualifying or apologizing for your projects. If you convey confidence, people will be less likely to judge or question you. They'll pick up on your enthusiasm and they might even mirror it and ask you to tell them more about your amazing projects.

Give Them Time to Come Around

I made sure to ask every single person I interviewed for this book about their upbringing. Did they have supportive parents who accepted their multipotentiality, or was it a struggle just to

---

7. One of the reasons I decided to do a TED talk was that I wanted multipotentialites to have a short resource they could send to their confused friends and family members.

8. If you don't feel very confident, it's okay to "fake it until you make it."

be who they are? Even if they stated that they didn't have their family's support early on, almost every one of my interviewees told me that their parents came around eventually. Once their loved ones saw that they were happy and financially stable, they backed off. They sometimes even became quite proud of all the interesting work their child was doing (even if they didn't totally understand all of it).

When parents encourage their kids to specialize, it usually comes from a place of love. They want their children to be self-sufficient, and specialization seems like a safe path to a well-paying job. Older generations don't always understand how different the economy is now and how important it has become to be adaptable and well versed. You can point them to the *Fast Company* article about "Generation Flux," which explains this cultural shift. You can list prominent figures who do many different things (Elon Musk, James Franco, Russell Simmons, Oprah Winfrey, Steve Martin, etc. See Appendix A for other famous multipotentialites.). You can try to explain that folks in the upper levels of corporations (COOs, directors, project managers, etc.) are usually generalists. But you might not want to play this game. It is often more effective to just wait it out, focus on building *your* multipotentialite life, and let your family members come around in their own time.

Ditch the Doubters

It is said that an individual is the product of her five closest friends. The people we choose to surround ourselves with profoundly impact our motivation, our goals, and what we believe is possible. Don't be afraid to step away from friendships and seek out new friends who have lifestyles and beliefs that are more aligned with the direction you want to move in. You aren't obligated to hang out with anybody you don't want to hang out with, especially people who are critical of your life choices or are negative in general. It can be hard to let go of friends you've had for most of your life, but sometimes it's the best option for mental and emotional health. Once you've ditched the doubters, it's time to . . .

Seek Out Supportive Community

Look for the multipotentialites in your life and deepen your relationship with them. Get online and seek out groups of artists, entrepreneurs, or others who are doing their own thing. You're always welcome to join our community at Puttylike.com, where you will meet a supportive group of multipotentialites who want to connect with other multipotentialites.

Believe in Your Right to Be Who You Are

You can, and should, try to explain your multipotentiality to the important people in your life. They might get it after a few conversations and some resources, or they might need more time to come around. But whether or not your family and friends approve, you need to live your life and do your thing. Get out there, start pursuing the areas that fascinate you, and find your people.

HOW TO ANSWER THE DREADED, "SO, WHAT DO YOU DO?"

You're at a party and your friend introduces you to a group of people. You know it's coming . . . that dreaded question: *So, what do you do?* Most of us hate being asked what we do. I mean, how do you introduce yourself when you might assume a dozen different roles on a regular basis and what you do is constantly changing? Unlike most people, you probably don't have one easy-to-explain job title or there might not be a single company that you can say you work for. Alternatively, you could have a job that brings in the majority of your income, but that job in no way encapsulates everything you do or what you are working toward. *What do you do?* is sort of like the adult version of *What do you want to be when you grow up?* Multipotentialites tend to have a very hard time answering it. How can we answer this awful but unavoidable question?

Context Is Everything: Tailor Your Answer to Who's Asking

Where are you, and who's asking the question? Are you at a party or social gathering that isn't industry-specific? Are you talking with someone who works in a field related to one of your passions? Are you a friend's plus-one at the annual Accountants' Ball?[9] Is the setting casual or professional? Is the person asking the question a potential new friend who seems

9. I'm pretty sure the Accountants' Ball needs to exist, if it doesn't already.

open-minded, or are they someone who's just trying to be polite? Once you decide how comfortable you feel, and whether it would be helpful/appropriate to go into the details, you can choose how you would like to respond.

In general, you can handle this question in two ways:

1. You can respond with a one-liner that might not encompass everything you do but is easy to understand (e.g., "I'm a marine biologist," or "I work at Google").

2. You can respond with a less conventional but more accurate answer that will likely lead to a conversation.

The decision to drop a quick one-liner or to engage in a conversation will depend on whom you're speaking with and how you're feeling. Do you feel like opening up to this person? Are you in the mood to dive in and talk about the many things you're about or would you prefer to move along with your day?

It's okay to have multiple answers to the question and to pick the one that is most appropriate for the occasion. If you choose to drop a short and easy-to-understand job title, don't worry if it doesn't convey the full spectrum of who you are. People can discover the other facets of your personality as they get to know you better.

The "I Do Many Things" Approach

If you're up for getting into a deeper conversation, you can lead with your multipotentiality. You can say something like "I do many things," or "I've got a bunch of different projects on the go right now," or even "I'm a multipotentialite!" This is probably the most genuine way to answer, but will definitely confuse people at first and require some explaining. However, if you sense that you might be in the company of another multi-potentialite or are just feeling excited about all your projects and want to talk about them, then it's a good way to go. And if you have a good enough job[10] that doesn't reflect everything you do, you can say something like, "I work at [company name] but there are a lot of other things that I'm involved in." The "I do many things" approach will lead to a discussion, so make sure you're up for talking about your various projects.

Using an Umbrella Title

Is there a broader term or category that encompasses much of what you do? For instance, instead of responding with "I'm an actor and painter and musician," you could say, "I'm an artist." Or instead of saying "I'm a geography teacher, a docent at the zoo, and a health coach," you could call yourself an educator. It can be helpful to write down your work and/or priority projects and think of a few umbrella titles that could encapsulate these different identities.

"I Help _____ Do _____."

Another option is to leave your medium/title out entirely and in-stead, talk about the people you help and what you accomplish

10. We discussed good enough jobs in Chapter 6.

through your work. If you were to say, "I help youth feel empowered," that doesn't mention the specifics about *how* you empower youth. Maybe you're a dance teacher, maybe you're a motivational speaker, maybe you work at a nonprofit that provides health services to homeless youth, or maybe you do all three. If they're interested in learning more about what you do, they'll ask, and then you can elaborate and get into the specifics.

Use This Question as a Filter

If someone asks you what you do and doesn't react well to your answer, then perhaps they are failing the interview to be your new buddy. Highlighting your multipotentiality can be a litmus test to help you determine whether to pursue a friendship with someone. You never know, sometimes being honest about your complexity will encourage the other person to open up about theirs. You might even find that you're speaking to another multipotentialite!

———————————

On a bad day, it's easy to think that it would be nice to explore our many interests in private while the rest of the world just let us be. But secluding ourselves and relegating our multipotentiality to the private sphere would be a disservice to us and to everyone else. Being an "out and proud" multipotentialite means interacting with the world, learning to talk about our work, and listening to our hearts in the face of fear or disapproval. It's not always easy or comfortable to show up as our whole selves. But doing it, together, is how we build a movement. Take a risk. Show the world how awesome you are and help lessen the stigma around doing many things. You'll feel better and you'll make it easier for other multipotentialites to be who they are.

CONCLUSION

In my third year of law school, I took a music policy class that changed the trajectory of my career. It was a small seminar: a handful of law, music, business, and arts students. The class revolved around a semester-long project. We were separated into interdisciplinary teams and asked to come up with an idea for a company that would challenge the business model of the mainstream music industry. This class was my actual dream. Not only did it touch on several topics I was interested in at the time—law, music, and entrepreneurship—but our team project was a glorious smoosh of perspectives and disciplines.

Feeling energized by the neat business idea we had concocted—an online arts collective of sorts—my teammates and I decided to submit our business plan to a university-wide entrepreneurial competition once the class had ended. A few weeks later, we found out that we had made it to the semifinals. We were ecstatic. The only problem was that we were now going to have to pitch the idea to a panel of *real* entrepreneurs and investors. If you've ever seen an episode of *Shark Tank* or *Dragons' Den,* that's a pretty accurate representation of what this thing was like.

In preparation for our big presentation, my teammates and I met with our professor and rehearsed our pitch for her. After listening closely, she offered us some constructive feedback. Then, noting our nerves, she said something that has stayed with me:

> Your project is weird. I don't mean that in a bad way. The idea is just very different from what the judges will be used to seeing. Don't hide that weirdness; feature it.

I knew she was talking about one presentation in one silly college competition, but I felt like I'd been given permission to do something I had never allowed myself to do: to **feature the things that make me unique**.

For most of my life, I'd been minimizing what makes me different: my multipotentiality, my opinions, my queerness, my physical presence. Whether it was my absolute refusal to raise my hand in class, the way I hid in my oversized skater clothes as a teenager, or my failure to mention my eclectic background to my colleagues in my twenties, I felt like my survival depended on blending in. Call it a result of childhood bullying or just what happens when you grow up in a culture that tells girls to make themselves small, but I wanted desperately to feel "normal," and I thought normal meant invisible. At the same time, there was an impulse inside of me that conflicted with allllll of that: my unflagging desire to express myself. This force won out when I wrote music, directed films, and otherwise made proactive choices in my life. But the two forces—the need to blend in and the need to stoke the creative flame inside—were at constant odds. My professor had given me a life-changing permission. It was not only okay to be my weird self; leading with my uniqueness might actually be the key to my success.

It turns out featuring our weirdness wasn't enough to win us the competition. We lost. Probably because we didn't *exactly* know how we would monetize the business. Oops. Our presentation was strong, though. More than that, I had fun, which was a small miracle. I had always despised public speaking (for obvious reasons), but this time I didn't try to be formal or put on a professional air. Sure, I was polished and prepared. But I also stayed my curious, subtly mischievous, enthusiastic self onstage. Emilie didn't disappear up there. She appeared. It felt amazing.

LEAD WITH YOUR MULTIPOTENTIALITY

Feature the things that make you unique has become a personal mantra and one of my Whys. Although I've done a lot of different things in my career, much of my last six years has been about helping others lead with what makes them unique—in this case, their multipotentiality.

What does it mean to lead with your multipotentiality? It isn't just about accepting and embracing your inner wiring. That's only the beginning. To lead with your multipotentiality is to build a *sustainable* life around your plurality. It means figuring out, in practical terms, how to get the **money, meaning,** and *variety* you require so that you can flourish, put your brilliance out into the world, and make it a better place.

Some multipotentialites attain the money, meaning, and variety they require by combining their interests in a single but multifaceted Group Hug career. Some multipotentialites pair together a few part-time jobs or businesses that are very different from one another and possess a number of slashes between their interesting titles. Some Einsteins feel safest and most satisfied by meeting their financial needs through a single job or business and exploring on the side, sans financial pressure. Then there are the Phoenixes, with their magnificent reinventions every few years. These folks like going deeper into one area before they're ready for a change. And of course, we mustn't forget about all the hybrids: those who freely shift between or blend work models.

Sometimes I think we're all hybrids and that categories are just a psychological game we play to feel safe. Still, we need examples to learn from, frameworks to show us where to begin, and structures, if only so we can defy them later. I've said it before and I'll say it again: use the information in this book that works for you and leave the rest. Smoosh work models together. Try a new work model each year if that makes you happy. ***Experiment, iterate, and personalize all of this. It's your career. It's your life.***

Another part of *leading with your multipotentiality* is learning to balance your insatiable curiosity with your desire for progress. Find some productivity techniques that work for you and build your toolbox. You're bound to get in your own way at times; we all do. A bit of self-imposed structure can go a long way to help you advance your projects, explore voraciously, and make peace with your inner Resistance.

We began our journey together with a story about social pressure, misunderstanding, and shame. If you recall, I had bumped into an acquaintance from my past who was confused by one of my radical shifts in direction. I realize now that this person didn't mean to be rude. She just didn't understand what it means to be a multipotentialite and I didn't have the confidence or vocabulary to explain it to her. I hope you've begun to cultivate this confidence in yourself and that you feel better equipped to address the internal and external voices that could bring you down. More than that, I hope you see that you don't need to justify your choices to anyone. *What would your life be like if you gave yourself permission to be everything you wanted to be?* What could you create or solve if you were to lead with your abounding passions? I don't know. But I sure hope to find out.

JOIN THE COMMUNITY!

I created Puttylike.com to be a home for multipotentialites. It's a blog, a trove of helpful resources, and a place for multipotentialites to connect with one another. Join us, and let's build lives around our many passions together.

I'll see you there.

Your pal and fellow multipotentialite,

Emilie

FAMOUS MULTIPOTENTIALITES

Maya Angelou (1928–2014): Memoirist, poet, civil rights activist, historian, dancer, musician, actor, performer, filmmaker, director, composer, scriptwriter, and professor.

David Bowie (1947–2016): Musician, actor, poet, playwright, painter, art collector, and costume designer. Bowie reinvented himself several times over the course of his musical career with a variety of personas and musical styles.

Richard Branson (b. 1950): Entrepreneur, investor, and philanthropist. He founded the Virgin Group, which owns over four hundred companies in fields as diverse as music, aerospace, and communications.

Ray Eames (1912–1988) *and Charles Eames* (1907–1978): A married couple and dynamo professional team who made significant contributions to modern architecture and furniture. They also worked in industrial and graphic design, fine arts, and film.

Tim Ferriss (b. 1977): Author, entrepreneur, and speaker who has written books about work, health, and learning. He holds a Guinness world record in tango and is a national Chinese kickboxing champion.

James Franco (b. 1978): Actor, director, film producer, painter, poet, writer, multimedia artist, musician, and teacher. Interesting side note: Franco narrated a documentary about Charles and Ray Eames. So many levels of multipotentiality going on there!

Benjamin Franklin (1706–1790): Author, printer, political theorist, politician, scientist, inventor, civic activist, and diplomat. Franklin helped draft the Declaration of Independence and the U.S. Constitution, invented bifocal glasses and the lightning rod, and organized the first successful American lending library.

Galileo Galilei (1564–1642): Astronomer, physicist, engineer, philosopher, and mathematician who played a major role in the scientific revolution of the seventeenth century.

Steve Jobs (1955–2011): Entrepreneur, inventor, and industrial designer, best known for cofounding Apple. Jobs revolutionized several industries, including personal computing, music, and animation.

Hedy Lamarr (1914–2000): Film actress and inventor. At the beginning of World War II, Lamarr developed a jam-proof radio guidance system for torpedoes. The navy used the technology during the Cuban missile crisis in 1962, and her design is still used in the communication technology industry.

Beatrix Potter (1866–1943): Writer, illustrator, natural scientist, and conservationist. Best known as the author of the children's book *The Tale of Peter Rabbit*. She also studied and painted fungi and was well respected in the field of mycology. Potter was a prizewinning breeder of Herdwick sheep and a farmer who was interested in land preservation.

Russell Simmons (b. 1957): Entrepreneur, producer, author, activist, and philanthropist. He cofounded the hip-hop music label Def Jam Recordings, created three clothing fashion lines, including Phat Farm, and co-owns a nonprofit organization that provides arts education programs to inner-city students.

Patti Smith (b. 1946): Musician, poet, memoirist, and visual artist. She was a highly influential figure in the New York City punk rock scene in the 1970s. Smith works in several artistic mediums and is known as the "punk poet laureate" for her fusion of rock and poetry.

EXAMPLES OF INTERDISCIPLINARY FIELDS

One of the ways multipotentialites cultivate variety in our careers is working in interdisciplinary fields. (See Chapter 4.) Below is a sampler of interdisciplinary fields that might be a good fit for multipotentialites. Keep in mind, there are thousands of interdisciplinary fields and new fields constantly emerging. Try not to get discouraged if you don't find a perfect fit in this list. There are blank spaces too—keep adding!

Field	Elements
Artificial Intelligence	Psychology, philosophy, technology, neuroscience, computer science, mathematics, robotics, pattern recognition, machine learning, visual perception
Bioethics	Life sciences, technology, medicine, politics, law, philosophy

Field	Elements
Bioinformatics	Computer science, biology, mathematics, statistics, engineering, UX design
Creative Coding	Programming, video, visual art, design, performance art, installations, sound, advertising, product prototypes
Design	Art, engineering, sociology, psychology, music, video, business, and subject related to each specific project
Education	Public speaking, leadership, learning styles, psychology, child development, counseling, management, specific subject matter(s)
Event Management	Project management, psychology, law, culture, business, finance, gastronomy, interior design
Filmmaking	Writing, storytelling, photography, art direction, technology, editing, sound, project management, business, law
Human Geography	Geography, anthropology, history, culture, research, economy, environmental policy
Instructional Design	Education theory, neuroscience, technology, interactive media design, psychology, research, storytelling, communications, programming, film, gamification, visual design, web design, audio production, technical writing, editing
Integrative Medicine	Western medicine, alternative medicine, herbalism, acupuncture, bodywork, nutrition, counseling, fitness, yoga, meditation
Marketing	Writing, design, statistics, data analysis, research, business, psychology, economics, project management, communications, technology

Field	Elements
Psychotherapy/Counseling	Psychology, listening, empathy, business; easily combined with other subjects (e.g., art therapy, music therapy, equine therapy, horticulture therapy, ocean therapy, yoga therapy)
Publishing	Language, communications, storytelling, layout, design, photography, technology, research, finance, law, business, management, teaching, "ideation," marketing
Sustainable Development	Organizational development, economics, social justice, ecology, politics, technology, business, architecture, culture
Urban Planning	Housing, transportation, environment, education, arts, agriculture, economics, architecture, design, landscape, civil engineering, social justice, public administration, history, research, mapping, writing, communications, law
User Experience (UX)	Coding, research, storytelling, design, visual art, technology, sociology, cultural studies, writing, communication, psychology, project management

ACKNOWLEDGMENTS

This book wouldn't have been possible without the support and wisdom of several rad multipotentialites (and some rad non-multipotentialites, too).

Puttypeep, and everyone in the Puttylike community—this movement would not exist without you. You have inspired me endlessly and taught me so much. I can't thank you enough for your feedback, ideas, and friendship over the years. I wrote this book to be *ours* and with my responsibility to all of you front and center in my heart.

My profound thanks to my editor, Hilary Lawson, and to everyone at HarperOne, especially Sydney Rogers, Kim Dayman, Adia Colar, and Noël Chrisman for your hard work and unwavering enthusiasm. Hilary, I couldn't have asked for a more wonderful editor. You've championed this book from the beginning, and your support, guidance, and openness made the daunting task of writing a book a (mostly) joyful one.

Thank you to my agent, Allison Hunter, and to everyone at the Stuart Krichevsky Agency and Janklow and Nesbit. Allison, thank you for your confidence, your advocacy, the fun brainstorms, and showing me the ropes in the big city!

So much gratitude to the amazing multipotentialites I interviewed and surveyed. You added such richness to this book. Your time and your stories mean the world to me.

Mom and Dad, thank you for letting me explore to my heart's content and for teaching me that learning has inherent value.

There are so many friends, family members, and colleagues who helped this book come about in obvious and less obvious ways. Jason Moore, Ethan Waldman, Diane Pauley, Joel Zaslofsky, Joanna James-Lynn, Neil Hughes, Jon Knepper, Rami Nuseir, Abe Cajudo, and Mike Pumphrey: y'all are my fam (or my "nerds" as Valerie would put it). Meeting you has been the best thing about my blogging journey. Special thanks, too, to Pamela Slim, Chris Guillebeau, Barbara Sher, Cheryl Dolan, Whitney Otto, Joy Harris, Margaux Yiu, Tim Manley, Melea Seward, Arianne Cohen Cozi, Brian Burk, Nora Brooks, Anne Rasmussen, William Anthony, Brigitte Lyons, Maggie Hassler, Tina Piper, Nisha Nathani, the teams at TED and TEDxBend, Stef, Varley, Stuart, and Al.

Finally there's Valerie, who spent too much time editing early drafts of this book for style, substance, and sass. This was such a collaboration—I couldn't have done it without you. You make my life so much easier and so much fuller. Thank you for your infinite love, encouragement, cleverness, and patience. I really am the luckiest.

NOTES AND
SELECTED FURTHER READING

CHAPTER 1

"Existential Depression in Gifted Individuals" by James Webb http://sengifted.org/existential-depression-in-gifted-individual.

CHAPTER 2

A cool article about transferable skills: "Neither Teaching nor Publishing: Post-M.F.A. Jobs Beyond Writing," http://www.publishersweekly.com/pw/by-topic/authors/mfa/article/68398-fall-2015-m-f-a-update-neither-teaching-nor-publishing-post-m-f-a-jobs-beyond-writing.html.

Adam Grant's quote is from: "How to Raise a Creative Child. Step One: Back Off," http://www.nytimes.com/2016/01/31/opinion/sunday/how-to-raise-a-creative-child-step-one-back-off.html.

CHAPTER 3

Marianna Virtanen and her colleagues at the Finnish Institute of Occupational Health have conducted numerous studies on the effects of overworking, including, "Long Working Hours and Cognitive Function: The Whitehall II Study" (2009), "Long Working Hours, Socioeconomic Status, and the Risk of Incident Type 2 Diabetes" (2015), and "Long Working Hours and Risk of Coronary Heart Disease and Stroke" (2015).

To learn more about the ingredient approach to money and for a smart look at personal finances, check out John Armstrong's book *How to Worry Less About Money,* which is published as part of the School of Life's self-help series.

CHAPTER 5

For a comprehensive look at the Slash Approach, check out *One Person / Multiple Careers* by Marci Alboher.

CHAPTER 6

Barbara Sher wrote about good enough jobs and scanners in *Refuse to Choose!*

CHAPTER 7

The loathing scale can be found in Pamela Slim's book *Body of Work* (note: she has a section about multipotentialites in her book!).

Learn more about doing free work in Charlie Hoehn's *Recession-Proof Graduate*.

CHAPTER 8

The Headspace meditation app can be found at headspace.com.

The concept of "Shitty First Drafts" is discussed in Anne Lamott's *Bird by Bird*.

CHAPTER 9

Amanda Palmer has a great discussion of imposter syndrome (which she calls "the fraud police") in her wonderful book, *The Art of Asking*.

This great *Fast Company* article looks at the importance of adaptability in the new world of work: "This Is Generation Flux: Meet the Pioneers of the New (and Chaotic) Frontier of Business," https://www.fast company.com/1802732/generation-flux-meet-pioneers-new-and-chaotic -frontier-business.

INDEX